MW00962748

Instructor's Manual and Test Bank to Accompany

Dimensions of Communication
An Introduction

Michele S. Hunkele
California Polytechnic State University–San Luis Obispo

Michael D. Scott
California State University-Chico

Steven R. Brydon
California State University-Chico

Mayfield Publishing Company
Mountain View, California
London • Toronto

Copyright © 1997 by Mayfield Publishing Company

All rights reserved. No portion of this book may be reproduced in any form or by any means without written permission of the publisher. Inclusion of a product or organization in the list of resources in this manual does not indicate an endorsement by Mayfield Publishing. Mayfield does not guarantee the accuracy of information in the products listed.

International Standard Book Number 1-55934-443-1

Manufactured in the United States of America

10   9   8   7   6   5   4   3   2   1

Mayfield Publishing Company
1280 Villa Street
Mountain View, California 94041
(415) 960-3222

INTRODUCTION

WELCOME TO TEACHING AN EXCITING AND CHALLENGING COURSE

Dimensions of Communication introduces interesting and relevant information on communication studies to students from all majors. This accompanying instructor's manual is a guide to assist you in teaching the material from *Dimensions of Communication* in what generally proves to be a fun but challenging course to teach.

A communication class that surveys many communication topics, in addition to providing students with practical public speaking experience, tends to be fast-paced. As you know or may imagine, adequate organization and preparation prove to be crucial elements for success.

We teach our students that communication competence is on a continuum, that we may be strong in some areas and need assistance in others. Likewise, instructors may have strengths and weaknesses based on variables such as experience or lack thereof and time constraints. As a result, this instructor's manual is a valuable resource. Included within this manual are key elements to classroom instruction: sample syllabi; evaluation tools; teaching and learning objectives; outlines; potential problem areas; instructional exercises; discussion topics; and test questions. They can be used when and if needed in their entirety or individually. Furthermore, when using this resource, keep in mind our understanding that the most effective teachers never stop learning and adapting material to better suit their teaching style, classroom environment, and students' individual and collective personalities. As a result, this manual should be viewed as a strong starting point, the beginning of a brainstorming session between one instructor and another.

You may be a new teacher or a teacher who has taught public speaking, small group communication, and hybrid classes for some time and decided to adopt a new text for more up-to-date research and/or a personal change. Regardless, you have adopted a text that is rich with relevant and interesting material. Good luck in your academic year!

HOW TO BEST USE THIS GUIDE

No two teachers will organize and prepare for class in exactly the same way. However, most effective classes have certain elements in common. This manual aims to provide you with those basic elements needed to make your class rewarding, for both you and your students.

Part One includes relevant information and suggestions on how to organize your class incorporating your text, *Dimensions of Communication*. In addition, many practical teaching tips based on the authors', Dr. Michael D. Scott's and Dr. Steven R. Brydon's, experiences in addition to my own, are provided.

Specifically, Part One includes:

- Helpful teaching tips

- Suggestions for organizing your class, including sample syllabi

- Providing evaluation and feedback, including sample evaluation forms

Part Two includes chapter-by-chapter items. For each chapter you may refer to:

- Chapter outlines
  Each chapter includes an extended outline. This outline provides a basis for lectures
  and a reference for key concepts introduced in students' reading.

- Teaching/learning objectives
  At the start of each chapter in *Dimensions of Communication*, Scott and Brydon list
  learning objectives which primarily focus students to increase their cognitive
  (intellectual) and psychomotor (performance) abilities and skills. In this manual,
  teaching/learning objectives provide instructors with goals for affective outcomes.
  Affective outcomes translate to students positively changing attitudes and behaviors
  on the material presented, in short, often because of the way that it is presented. The
  final objective refers you back to the equally important learning objectives based on
  students' reading.

- Troubleshooting items
  When teaching a course that introduces basic human communication theory and
  requires public speaking and group interaction, instructors may encounter a variety
  of obstructions to students' learning. Many potential stumbling blocks are addressed
  in this section, although, given the uniqueness of each classroom, others could arise.

- Instructional exercises
  A number of activities provide instructors with the opportunity to break away from
  traditional lectures. The exercises provided invite students to reflect on their own
  experiences and interact with classmates. Engaging in instructional exercises
  reinforces the ideas that communication is a transaction and a learned skill.

- Journal writing
  Including journal writing in your classroom is an optional activity. This section
  offers suggested writing topics that may be graded or nongraded, collected,
  shared in class, or shared within small groups.

- Discussion topics
  Relevant discussion and debate breathes life into the material presented on the pages
  in *Dimensions of Communication*. Potential discussion topics are provided.

- Multiple choice, true/false, and short answer/essay test questions allow you to
  test students in whatever format is best suited to your particular class setting.

CONTENTS

PART ONE
ORGANIZING THE COURSE

HELPFUL TEACHING TIPS

REMEMBER: STUDENTS LEARN BY SEEING, HEARING, AND DOING

When you are preparing for class, it is important to keep in mind that students have different modes of learning. Information should be presented incorporating methods which appeal to all students.

"Seeing" may include activities such as

- watching the video whenever appropriate,
- requiring that students observe and evaluate other students' performances,
- becoming a model communicator yourself,
- collecting and sharing relevant examples from day-to-day encounters,
- using audiovisual materials such as overhead transparencies and PowerPoint.

"Hearing" may include activities such as

- engaging the classroom in discussion,
- presenting traditional lectures,
- bringing in music in which the lyrics demonstrate a point,
- incorporating other auditory messages from the countless daily messages we receive.

"Doing" may include activities such as

- engaging students in instructional exercises presented in this manual,
- providing students with numerous opportunities to practice communication skills,
- facilitating your class in such a way that all students are required to mentally answer every question asked by you. For example, some instructors ask all students to stand after asking a question. Students are instructed not to sit until they are prepared to answer. This way, technically, all students are ready to be called upon and have actively engaged in learning.

MAKE GOOD USE OF THE FIRST DAY OF CLASS

Often the most important day of class is the first one. Impressions are formed that may take a whole semester to change. The instructor who comes to the first class unprepared, who seems disorganized, and who either wastes the class's time or lets everyone go after a few minutes is setting a tone that will be difficult to overcome.

Teachers should make good use of the first day of class. The semester, and most definitely the quarter, offer limited time to cover all the material and complete all the necessary presentations. On a productive first day:

- **Handle all procedural matters.** Attendance needs to be taken, and depending on your university's policy, you may be required to add or drop students. Consider that many students will want to add a class, and that physical space may still be available, after the official maximum number have been enrolled. Be prepared to explain to students that in order for you to effectively teach and students to successfully complete the course, only a limited number of students can be enrolled.

- **Explain the syllabus.** The syllabus serves as a contract between the student and teacher. It should be sufficiently detailed to outline all course requirements, answer students' concerns, and reduce their uncertainties about the class. More information on creating your syllabus appears in the "Suggestions for Organizing Your Class" section of this manual.

- **"Sell" yourself and your class.** Motivate students by explaining how the knowledge and skills gained in this class will help them to meet their personal and professional goals. Present yourself in the most professional and credible light as possible. Outline your credentials and provide some personal, but not too personal, information as well.

- **Show students their textbook.** Bring a copy of the text to class and promote its value to the class. Most students do not enjoy spending money on texts and spending their out-of-class time reading. As a result, you must ensure students of the text's worth. Instruct those students who have not already purchased it where to do so and the cost. Handle any backorder or out-of-stock issues. It's a good idea to have a copy available on reserve in the library in case a student cannot legitimately afford to buy the text. In addition, a reading assignment may be assigned to immediately engage students in the term's activities.

- **Explain your expectations to the class.** Students need to know at a very personal level what you expect of them. Likewise, it may prove helpful to inquire about what students expect from you and the class. This may be done in an open discussion or through a written questionnaire. If you have any pet peeves or idiosyncratic rules, clearly inform students at this time.

- **Begin getting to know your students as individuals.** If time permits, incorporate an ice-breaking activity. At minimum, have brief introductions and begin to learn all students' names.

INCORPORATE THE VIDEO IN ORDER TO USE CLASS TIME WISELY

Dimensions of Communication provides a wealth of relevant and interesting material for students. Yet, covering all 18 chapters and incorporating presentations will prove to be challenging for even the most effective time managers. Thus, *Dimensions of Communication* is an integrated package of text and video that saves the instructor class time. When you adopt both the text and the video, students gain access to sample speeches, speech critiques, interviews with experts, and a number of other segments. You can also use the video in the classroom to introduce a topic with high impact and in a succinct manner or outside of the classroom by students individually or in groups.

CREATE AN EFFECTIVE CLASSROOM CLIMATE

Public speaking ranks first among 40% of all adults' lists of fears. Negative past small group experiences may haunt students. As a result, many students are predisposed to be apprehensive or experience what is commonly called communication anxiety.

The classroom climate sets the overall tone for the class. What is comfortable and uncomfortable for students to say and/or practice is a direct result of the classroom climate. Creating a climate that is conducive to learning and psychologically safe should be a primary goal of the instructor.

BE SENSITIVE TO STUDENT DIFFERENCES

It is important to be sensitive to students' differences, whether based on cultural, group, or individual diversity. As discussed in Chapter 7, all three levels of diversity are important forms of data when adapting to the rhetorical situation and aiming to engage in diversity-responsive communication. Learn about your students' cultural, group, and individual differences, and encourage them to share these differences with their classmates. Briefly consider each level:

- **Cultural** It is particularly important in today's diverse classrooms to be sensitive to cultural differences. Culture is the collective pattern of thinking, feeling, and acting characteristic of a specific human society.

- **Group** Here we are concerned with groups to which students belong that help them to shape how they experience and interpret their world. Groups may include: the geographic region they refer to as "home"; race and ethnicity; gender; religion; socioeconomic class; generation; and campus organizations such as fraternities, sororities, and interest-based groups.

- **Individual** Individual diversity is deeply embedded in our personal beliefs, attitudes, and values. It is these individual variables that make each student unique.

SUGGESTIONS FOR ORGANIZING YOUR CLASS

CREATE A CLEAR, COMPLETE, AND REALISTIC SYLLABUS

The syllabus serves as a contract between the student and teacher. Therefore, if you expect students to follow the terms of the agreement, then you too must fulfill your end of the bargain. A dropped assignment may please some, but disappoint others who were counting on it to raise their grade. With this in mind, it is important that your syllabus be clear and complete, yet realistic. Following are sample syllabi for teaching this course on both the semester and quarter system. You may choose to adopt them as they are or adapt them to better fit your style. If you create your own syllabus, consider including the following information:

- Course information which includes
  - Title of course
  - Time and place of meeting
  - Course catalog description
  - Course prerequisites
- Instructor information which includes
  - Name and title of instructor
  - Instructor's office hours, location, and phone number
- Course goals and objectives
- Required textbook (full source citation) and other required materials
- Course requirements to successfully complete the class which may include specifics about
  - Attendance
  - Assignments
  - Exams
  - Participation
  - Academic honesty
  - Grading standards
- Course policies regarding
  - Absences and tardiness
  - Makeups
  - Extra credit
  - Academic honesty
- Grading system
- Session-by-session class calendar which includes lecture topics, due dates for all assignments, exam dates, and vacation dates

SCHEDULE SPEAKING DATES

You may arbitrarily assign speaking dates or allow students to sign up for days that work best for them. Regardless of your method, a clear speaking schedule for individual and group presentations is essential to maintaining a well-organized class. Plan the semester or quarter well enough in advance that all speaking dates are known to everyone from the onset. You may also choose to determine speaking order in addition to speaking date.

If you choose to allow students to sign up, students can potentially avoid any conflicts with additional assignments or their personal commitments. Furthermore, this method requires students to take responsibility for swapping their speaking date with another student or group in the event of a conflict.

Creating a fair method for sign-ups proves challenging. Inevitably the last to sign up will become one of the first to speak. With this in mind, create a system which is fair but does not cost too much valuable classroom time. Suggestions include:

- **Create a lottery system.** If there are 25 students in your class, write the numbers 1–25 on individual pieces of paper in a bag. For each speech, have students draw a number. Number one gets first choice of date (and potentially speaking order on that date) and so on. Adapt this system to work for group presentations.

- **Create separate sign up sheets for each speech and pass them around beginning at different points in the classroom.** When using this for group sign ups, be sure to instruct group members to get together so that they can collectively decide.

- **Create speaking groups and rotate the order.** Divide the class or use the small groups designated for small group activities. Group A speaks first on the first speech but last on the next speech, fourth on the next, and so on. With five speeches and five groups, no one group is disadvantaged. This system works best when you have an even number of groups and individual/group presentations.

- **Display sign-up sheets outside of your office.** Be sure not to sign up too many speakers for any given class period. Keep in mind some of the following variables which are discussed in more detail later:
  - setting up the video equipment if you elect to tape speeches;
  - assigning speaking order if not predetermined;
  - assigning student critiques;
  - providing some immediate feedback;
  - students who ignore time requirements;
  - attending to "housekeeping" items such as returning assignments.

ORGANIZE THE SPEAKING ORDER

Organizing the speaking order on a given day can be handled by having students sign up to speak in a given order, asking for volunteers, or using the "sign-in" system. To use the sign-in system, first put a list of numbers on the board corresponding to the number of speakers on a given day. Then, students sign up for their preferred speaking positions as they arrive.

ASSIGN STUDENT CRITICS

Among other things, becoming a competent communicator requires (1) giving feedback and (2) observing another's behavior and deciding which skills to add to or omit from one's own repertoire. Thus, it is important to require students to offer evaluations of at least one speaker on presentation days. You may choose to excuse those who are giving individual or group presentations from critiquing since they will already have much to think about.

There are many ways to assign critics and many tools to use for evaluation. See the sample critique forms in the "Providing Evaluation and Feedback" section. Ways to assign critics include:

- Using the above sign-in method for organizing speaking order, simply have students count off by the number of students speaking that day. From the list on the board they can determine who they are evaluating. For example, if five students are scheduled to speak, all students count off 1, 2, 3, 4, 5, and all the 1s evaluate the first speech, the 2s the second, and so forth.

- Using the sign-up sheets, predetermine who will critique whom on what day. Using a sign-up sheet from any given day, be sure that all those in the class not included are assigned to critique someone scheduled to speak. Announce the critiquing order at the start of the class, or create a handout that indicates students' critiquing responsibilities for the entire semester or quarter.

- Create a buddy system. Have students pair off and commit to critiquing one another for all presentations. This allows at least one other person to chart a student's progress throughout the term. Use the buddy system in addition to any other method to ensure that students receive feedback from more than one student.

SET CLEAR TIME LIMITS

Given the amount of information that needs to be covered and the number of presentations that must be completed in a term, setting clear time limits for all activities and presentations is essential.

If you plan to penalize students for shorting or exceeding a time limit in individual or group presentations, your policy must be clearly explained.

When creating your policy, be sure to consider the following:

- How many points will be deducted?

- Whose responsibility will it be to inform the speaker of his or her time? Will you provide visual time cues or expect the student to use his or her own watch while you use your own?

- Will you interrupt a speaker if he or she continues speaking past a certain time?

BALANCE PROVIDING OPPORTUNITIES FOR PUBLIC SPEAKING PRACTICE WITH COVERING OTHER RELEVANT INFORMATION

Instructors need to balance covering the material presented in 18 chapters with providing students time to practice the skills they read about. Here lies the challenge.

When preparing for class and deciding how to best expend limited time, instructors should keep in mind first that this may be the only communication class these students will ever take. Therefore, instructors have the challenge of at least introducing, and hopefully exciting students about, the numerous dimensions of communication. Students also need opportunities to practice these skills in your class so that they have increased ability when they leave at the end of the semester or quarter.

In a class that aims to teach public speaking as well as small group interaction, opportunities for individual and group presentations must be provided. One way to ensure that students cover the text material and gain practice is to assign presentations that discuss information presented in the text. For example, individual presentations could include informative speeches on how to dress for an interview. Or as a group presentation, students may be required to inform students about family communication, using Chapter 9 as a foundation. After the presentations are complete, the instructor may add any key ideas that the individual or group may have missed, and then it can be considered covered material for testing purposes.

In a class that focuses on communication, all presentations can easily be tied to communication. In fact you may encourage students to explore how communication affects them in order to reinforce the idea that communication pervades our lives. For example, informative speeches may include topics on communication inventions such as the telephone or printing press or how to surf the Internet. Persuasive speeches could range from the power of advertising to the debate over the V-chip.

Regardless of how you choose to facilitate instruction, remember that as a general rule of thumb, the less you talk and the more the students talk, the better.

DEVELOP TOOLS FOR EFFECTIVE EVALUATION

Students deserve to know the criteria upon which they will be evaluated either individually or as a group. Develop a tool that provides an opportunity to both acknowledge strengths and indicate areas which need improvement. At minimum, an effective evaluation tool lists all required organizational elements of the presentation, as well as any skills needed to deliver a presentation effectively. In the "Providing Evaluation and Feedback" section of this manual, sample evaluation forms for both individual and group presentations are provided.

HAVE STUDENTS SPEAK OFTEN AND EARLY

Given that most students dread public speaking but need to practice the skill, instructors should aim to have students speaking as frequently as possible. In fact, if time allows, have students begin practicing their public speaking skills on the first day of class. The following ice-breaking activities provide students with the opportunity to introduce themselves and begin to know their classmates. Keep in mind, the content of the introduction is less important than providing students with an opportunity to give their first "speech."

- Students will break into pairs consisting of strangers. Instruct students that without verbally communicating or providing any nonverbal feedback to their partner, they should write down the predictions about the person based on all available cues. Predictions should focus on the following:

- The geographic region they refer to as home
- Age
- Major
- Class standing
- Political preference
- Dating status
- Musical preference
- Hobbies/activities

After students have recorded their predictions, instruct students to introduce themselves to their partners and compare their predictions to the facts. Inform students that their task will be to introduce their partner and provide interesting information about him or her to the class. Encourage students to be creative and enthusiastic in their introductions. Have students introduce one another in pairs in the front of the class.

- Have students introduce themselves to the class by providing basic biographical information including name, major, home town, interests, and hobbies. In addition to providing this basic data, ask students to share one unique quality about themselves.

- Have students introduce themselves by stating their name, major, and ten adjectives that describe themselves. At the end of their introduction, instruct students to leave the audience with an alliteration device that will help others to remember their name. They should include one adjective that begins with the same letter as their first name (e.g., Serious Sam or Athletic Anne).

Consider the following impromptu exercises in instances where you have extra class time.

- In a 2–3-minute speech, have students explain something that irritates them. Are they bothered by smokers or nonsmokers, barking dogs, dorm food, noisy neighbors, phone-hogging roommates, other people's music, or gum cracking? Whatever it is, ensure students that this is their opportunity to "sound off." Instruct students to open their speech with impact, making the audience sit up and take notice of their pet peeve. In the body of their speech, they should develop some reasons why this bothers them, citing specific examples. Finally, they should close with impact.

- Divide students into pairs. Provide one student with one quote that seems to contradict the quote given to the other student. In a 2–3-minute speech, students should read the quote, explain why it is true, citing examples, and leave the audience with something to think about. Quote pairs should go to the front of the class together and take turns speaking. Following the speeches, ask audience members to vote for the speech that most accurately reflects their personal view. Possible quote pairs include:
  - Opposites attract vs. Birds of a feather flock together
  - There is no such thing as a free lunch vs. The best things in life are free
  - Absence makes the heart grow fonder vs. Out of sight, out of mind

- Collect unusual items from your home, garage, and office. Have students draw items from a paper bag. In a 2–3-minute speech, students must explain what this item is and its uses, real or imagined. Instruct students to follow the guidelines for effective speeches. Have audience members vote on whether or not they believe the speaker and his or her description.

INCREASE STUDENTS' UNDERSTANDING OF THE RESPONSIBILITIES OF BOTH THE SPEAKER AND LISTENER

In the communication transaction, both speakers and listeners have ethical responsibilities. Following are lists of responsibilities that you should stress to students. Any penalties for not living up to these responsibilities should be made explicitly clear.

Listener responsibilities dictate that students should

- Arrive in class on time.
- Pay undivided attention to the speaker.
- Avoid mentally tuning out the speaker if the speaker says something that is disagreeable.
- Applaud for speakers when they have completed their presentations.
- Avoid interrupting a speech already in progress. This may require instructing late classmates to remain outside the classroom door until they hear applause on presentation days.
- Provide constructive feedback in classroom discussions or on evaluation sheets.
- Ask questions in a nonconfrontational manner, when and if provided the opportunity.

Speaker responsibilities dictate that students should

- Arrive in class on time and prepared to give their presentation.
- Present information that is worthwhile to the audience.
- Present information in an understandable manner.
- Practice rhetorically sensitive communication.
- Respect time limits.
- Respond to audience feedback.

LIVE UP TO YOUR RESPONSIBILITIES AS INSTRUCTOR

An instructor's primary responsibility is to enhance learning. These are attitudes and actions I have made my personal responsibility in order to more successfully meet this challenge.

- Spend the necessary time to prepare fresh lectures. Use this instructor's manual as a resource.
- Demonstrate enthusiasm for the material you introduce.

- Provide students with clear goals, objectives, and criteria.
- Avoid unnecessary ambiguity.
- Provide constructive and timely feedback and evaluations.
- Follow through on commitments and promises.
- Regularly attend office hours and make yourself available to students who have scheduling conflicts.
- Get to know your students' names and use them.
- Show up for class on time and prepared.
- Pay undivided attention to your students when in the classroom.
- Be responsive to students' needs.
- Be fair.
- Admit when you've made a mistake.
- Create an effective classroom climate.

SAMPLE SYLLABI

COURSE NUMBER AND TITLE OF CLASS

Instructor:

Office:

Office Phone:

Office Hours:

COURSE DESCRIPTION AND OBJECTIVES

This course is a general education requirement and is designed to enable students to become more competent communicators. [You may want to include the university catalog description here.] This requires students to

- learn the basic principles of human communication;
- practice creating, organizing, and presenting effective messages;
- analyze communication situations, audiences, and purposes;
- become a more critical thinker and listener; and
- understand your relationship and ethical responsibilities to others involved in communication transactions.

TEXTBOOK AND OTHER REQUIRED MATERIAL

Scott, M. D., & Brydon, S. R. (1996). *Dimensions of Communication*. Mountain View, CA: Mayfield.

One VHS videotape.

CLASS REQUIREMENTS

This class will require students to satisfactorily complete

- chapter readings,
- two graded speeches (including written outlines),
- two group presentations,
- two exams, and
- class participation activities.

Chapter readings will be required to be completed before entering class. Periodic quizzes can be expected if it appears that students are not satisfactorily completing reading assignments. Refer to the class schedule for specific assignments.

Two graded speeches [These are suggested assignments.]

Speech one: A six-minute informative speech on a topic that informs fellow students about a communication concept or advance and/or demonstrates or describes how communication affects our everyday lives. One visual aid and a formal outline are required.

Speech two: An eight-minute persuasive speech on a current topic of your choice. One visual aid and a formal outline are required.

Two group presentations [These are suggested assignments. If you teach on the quarter system, these may need to be shortened due to limited class time.]

Presentation one:

- For the semester system, students are to prepare a panel discussion regarding a current event in the media. The length of the presentation is determined by the number of group members included. For each member add five minutes to the presentation length. Each member is responsible for one visual aid and an individual outline.

- For the quarter system, students are to become a formal social group and engage in a bonding activity. This activity should promote cohesiveness to assist you in fulfilling the requirements of your next group presentation. In your 8–10-minute presentation, explain who you are, what activity you engaged in, and what we can expect in your next presentation. At least one visual aid is required.

Presentation two:

- For the semester system, each group is to solve a community or university problem. In a two-part presentation, students are to explain the current problem and how it affects this particular audience. Next, they should present a plausible solution to the problem. The length of the presentation is determined by the number of group members included. For each member add five minutes to the presentation length. Each member is responsible for one visual aid and an individual outline.

- For the semester system, each group is to prepare an informative presentation on assigned chapter information from *Dimensions of Communication*. Groups are responsible for relaying all information in a balanced, creative, and organized manner. You will have a maximum of 35 minutes out of the 50-minute class period. Visual aids are optional. Each student is responsible for an individual outline and preparing three test questions that can be used to determine the effectiveness of delivering the material. These questions should be combined on one page and turned in the class period before your assigned speaking date.

Two exams are scheduled. The midterm and final will consist of 50 multiple choice and true/false items and five short essay questions. Test questions come from chapter readings and class lectures. Each students is responsible for bringing a scantron and blue book on test day.

Class participation activities include attendance; delivering nongraded speeches; participating in instructional exercises; critiquing classmates, presentations; writing journal entries; and any quizzes.

All written assignments must be typed and utilize standard source citation. Use the Modern Language Association (MLA) or American Psychological Association (APA) style guide. Both are available behind the reference desk in the library. All written work will be graded for content, form, and professionalism. No late assignments will be accepted. Academic honesty is expected. Students are expected to practice academic honesty, and I expect that it will not be a problem in this class. However, if you are unfamiliar with the rules of academic honesty, please request to see the university's guidelines.

ATTENDANCE AND MAKEUPS

Attendance in class is required. One becomes a competent communicator through: (1) understanding communication principles; (2) practicing these principles; and (3) observing these principles in the transactions of others. Take responsibility for your own learning. Come to class and come prepared. If you miss two or more class periods, without valid reasons, your participation grade will be impacted by 50%. There will be no makeups of exams, speeches, critiques, and class activities missed for unexcused absences. If you need to miss a class when you are scheduled to give an individual speech, you must find someone to switch places with you, except in the case of unforeseen events. Obviously, if you miss group presentations, there is no means to make up this part of your grade. If you anticipate any problems with exam dates, please talk to me before the exams so we can make arrangements.

GRADING

Final grades will be determined using the following [You may also choose to use a point system]:

- Informative Speech   15%
- Persuasive Speech   20%
- First Group Presentation*   10%
- Second Group Presentation*   10%
- Midterm Exam   15%
- Final Exam   20%
- Class Participation   10%

* Group presentations will be graded with a total 5% (or 50% of the grade) being an individual grade and the other 5% (or 50%) being a collective group grade.

DAILY COURSE SCHEDULE: 10-WEEK 40-HOUR QUARTER

(This sample syllabus is created assuming that your class meets three times weekly and has approximately 25 students enrolled. Furthermore, it is created emphasizing the need for balance between covering text material and providing students with the opportunities to speak early in the quarter and as often as possible. Be sure to check the university calendar to determine the actual number of class meetings in any given quarter.)

WEEK/DAY	CLASS TOPICS	ASSIGNMENTS DUE
Week One		
[Include actual dates if possible]		
Day 1	Class Introduction	
	Syllabus Review	
	Introduction Speeches	
Day 2	What Is Communication	
	and Communication Competence?	Chapter 1
Day 3	The Role of Perception	Chapter 2
Week Two		
Day 4	Verbal and Nonverbal Communication	Chapters 3 and 4
Day 5	Communication and Diversity	Chapter 7
Day 6	Preparing and Delivering Your	
	Speech Effectively	Chapter 14
Week Three		
Day 7	Nongraded Speeches	Chapter 15
Day 8	Nongraded Speeches	Speeches
Day 9	Informative Speaking and	Chapter 16
	Topic Brainstorming	
Week Four		
Day 10	Ethical Communication	Informative sign-up topic due and Chapter 5
Day 11	Critical Thinking and Listening	Chapter 6
Day 12	Persuasive Speaking	Persuasive sign-up and Chapter 17
Week Five		
Day 13	Midterm Exam	
Day 14	Informative Speeches	Work on informative and persuasive speeches
Day 15	Informative Speeches	

Week Six

Day 16	Informative Speeches	
Day 17	Informative Speeches and Introduction to Small Group Communication	Chapter 12
Day 18	Small Group Communication	Chapter 13

Week Seven

Day 19	Small Group Communication
Day 20	Small Group Presentations
Day 21	Persuasive Speeches

Week Eight

Day 22	Persuasive Speeches
Day 23	Persuasive Speeches
Day 24	Persuasive Speeches

Week Nine

Day 25	Small Group Presentations (Relational Communication)	Chapter 8
Day 26	Small Group Presentations (Family Communication)	Chapter 9
Day 27	Small Group Presentations (Relational Conflict)	Chapter 10

Week Ten

Day 28	Small Group Presentations (Interviewing)	Chapter 11
Day 29	Small Group Presentations (Mass Communication)	Chapter 18
Day 30	Review for the final	

DAILY COURSE SCHEDULE: 15-WEEK 45-HOUR QUARTER

(This sample syllabus is created assuming that your class meets three times weekly and has approximately 25 students enrolled. Furthermore, it is created emphasizing the need for balance between covering text material and providing students with the opportunities to speak early in the quarter and as often as possible. Be sure to check the university calendar to determine the actual number of class meetings in any given quarter.)

WEEK/DAY	CLASS TOPICS	ASSIGNMENTS DUE
Week One		
[Include actual dates if possible]		
Day 1	Class Introduction	
	Syllabus Review	
	Introduction Speeches	
Day 2	What Is Communication	
	and Communication Competence?	Chapter 1
Day 3	The Role of Perception	Chapter 2
Week Two		
Day 4	Communication and Language	Chapter 3
Day 5	Nonverbal Communication	Chapter 4
Day 6	Preparing and Delivering Your	
	Speech Effectively	Chapter 14
Week Three		
Day 7	Nongraded Speeches	Chapter 15
Day 8	Nongraded Speeches	
Day 9	Informative Speaking and	Chapter 16
	Topic Brainstorming	
Week Four		
Day 10	Creating Effective Visual Aids	Video segment
Day 11	Communication and Diversity	Chapter 7
Day 12	Ethical Communication	Informative sign-up/
		topic due and Chapter 5
Week Five		
Day 13	Critical Thinking and Listening	Chapter 6
Day 14	Persuasive Speaking	Chapter 17
Day 15	Persuasive Speaking	Persuasive sign-up
Week Six		
Day 16	Midterm Exam	
Day 17	Informative Speeches	Work on informative
		and persuasive speeches
Day 18	Informative Speeches	

Week Seven
Day 19   Informative Speeches   Chapter 12
Day 20   Informative Speeches
Day 21   Small Group Communication   Chapter 13

Week Eight
Day 22   Small Group Communication
Day 23   Small Group Communication
Day 24   Small Group Presentations

Week Nine
Day 25   Small Group Presentations
Day 26   Small Group Presentations
Day 27   Small Group Presentations

Week Ten
Day 28   Small Group Presentations
Day 29   Relational Communication   Chapter 8
Day 30   Family Communication   Chapter 9

Week Eleven
Day 31   Persuasive Speeches
Day 32   Persuasive Speeches
Day 33   Persuasive Speeches

Week Twelve
Day 34   Persuasive Speeches
Day 35   Relational Conflict   Chapter 10
Day 36   Interviewing   Chapter 11

Week Thirteen
Day 37   Impromptu/Nongraded Speeches
Day 38   Mass Communication   Chapter 18
Day 39   Small Group Presentations

Week Fourteen
Day 40   Small Group Presentations
Day 41   Small Group Presentations
Day 42   Small Group Presentations

Week Fifteen
Day 43   Small Group Presentations
Day 44   Semester Wrap-up
Day 45   Review for Final Exam

PROVIDING EVALUATION AND FEEDBACK

GIVE STUDENTS A CHANCE TO SPEAK WITHOUT WORRYING ABOUT GRADES

Students will feel more confident, and therefore will more likely succeed at public speaking, if they are provided opportunities to practice their skills in front of an audience without worrying about a grade. This doesn't mean that the assignment shouldn't be subject to critical evaluation. Instead, nongraded assignments provide students with an opportunity to receive valuable feedback from you regarding skill areas where they need to improve.

ALLOW STUDENTS TO MAKE MISTAKES EARLY AND REWARD IMPROVEMENT

Consider weighing early presentations as less significant in the overall grade than later ones. Also, you might keep individual notes on a student regarding skill areas that you have specifically requested that he or she work on.

DEVELOP CLEAR GRADING CRITERIA

It is unfair to grade students using ambiguous standards. Develop your evaluation tool and spend class time explaining what is expected of students to fulfill the criteria. Consider using the *Dimensions of Communication* videotape to review and evaluate sample speeches with your students in order to further clarify your expectations.

MAKE USE OF VIDEOTAPE

If students don't like what they see, then they will work to fix it. Using videotape in your class (1) provides students with an invaluable learning tool and (2) ultimately makes your job easier. Instructors often complain that they tell the same students to stop engaging in the same behavior over and over again. However, if instructors tape students' speeches, students can see for themselves what instructors are referring to and become their own critics. Having a videotape of student speeches also becomes useful in the event that a student disputes his or her grade.

PROVIDE ORAL FEEDBACK IN ADDITION TO WRITTEN FEEDBACK

There are different ways to provide oral feedback. They depend on your personal style and available time. Some instructors prefer to discuss each student's speech as it is completed for immediacy purposes. Others feel this is threatening to students and time consuming. Consider listening to a few or all speeches on a given day, and then discuss themes you observed. Using this method, you can highlight class strengths or point out areas that need improvement without singling out any one person. If time permits before closing class, engage the class in a general discussion of things that they liked and learned from all speeches and some areas that they noticed everyone could practice to improve.

PROVIDE WRITTEN EVALUATION IN A TIMELY MANNER

To provide student feedback, use a written evaluation tool that has been clearly explained to students. Ideally, you should aim to return student evaluations during the class period following any given presentation. At minimum, be sure that students receive feedback in enough time to improve trouble areas before delivering their next presentation. Sample evaluation forms for an individual and group presentation follow.

EFFECTIVE SPEAKING IMPROVEMENT WORKSHEET: STUDENT

Name of speaker: _____

Topic: _____

Name of evaluator: _____

5=outstanding, 4=above average, 3=average, 2=below average, 1=poor, NA=not applicable

Selection of topic	5	4	3	2	1	NA
Opens with impact	5	4	3	2	1	NA
Clear thesis	5	4	3	2	1	NA
Connects with audience	5	4	3	2	1	NA
Clear preview	5	4	3	2	1	NA
Clear main points	5	4	3	2	1	NA
Clear signposts	5	4	3	2	1	NA
Adequate supporting material	5	4	3	2	1	NA
Effective use of visual aids	5	4	3	2	1	NA
Effective language use	5	4	3	2	1	NA
Effective vocal delivery	5	4	3	2	1	NA
Maintains eye contact	5	4	3	2	1	NA
Natural gesture/posture	5	4	3	2	1	NA
Summarizes main points	5	4	3	2	1	NA
Concludes with impact	5	4	3	2	1	NA
Overall effectiveness	5	4	3	2	1	NA

Provide additional comments on back if needed.

EFFECTIVE SPEAKING IMPROVEMENT WORKSHEET: INSTRUCTOR

(Turn in to instructor before speaking)

Name of speaker: _____

Topic: _____

5=outstanding, 4=above average, 3=average, 2=below average, 1=poor, NA=not applicable

Selection of topic	5	4	3	2	1	NA
Opens with impact	5	4	3	2	1	NA
Clear thesis	5	4	3	2	1	NA
Connects with audience	5	4	3	2	1	NA
Clear preview	5	4	3	2	1	NA
Clear main points	5	4	3	2	1	NA
Clear signposts	5	4	3	2	1	NA
Adequate supporting material	5	4	3	2	1	NA
Effective use of visual aids	5	4	3	2	1	NA
Effective language use	5	4	3	2	1	NA
Effective vocal delivery	5	4	3	2	1	NA
Maintains eye contact	5	4	3	2	1	NA
Natural gesture/posture	5	4	3	2	1	NA
Summarizes main points	5	4	3	2	1	NA
Concludes with impact	5	4	3	2	1	NA
Overall effectiveness	5	4	3	2	1	NA

Speech Grade (minus time penalty if applicable):

Outline Grade:

Total Assignment Grade:

OUTLINE CHECKLIST

(To be attached to each outline turned in to instructor when outline is due)

Specific Purpose:

____ is not an infinitive phrase.

____ is too vague and general.

____ is missing.

Thesis statement:

____ is not a single, complete sentence.

____ does not adequately capture the central theme of your speech.

____ is missing.

Outline content:

____ Your outline is too skimpy ____/too extensive ____.

____ You overlook the requirement for complete sentences.

____ Your main points do not fully develop your thesis statement ___, or your subpoints do not fully develop your main points ____.

____ Your preview does not adequately forecast your main points.

____ Your signposts do not adequately introduce the next points.

____ Your summary does not accurately recap your main points.

____ Your citation of sources is:

inadequate ____/nonexistent ____/not in correct format ____.

Outline format:

____ You have not labeled:

introduction ____ , body ____ , and/or conclusion ____.

____ You have not labeled speech components (OPEN, THESIS, etc.).

____ You have more than one sentence per letter/number.

____ You omit standard outline notation ____ , indentation ____.

____ The outline does not meet college standards of composition (too many mechanical errors).

____ You omit preview ____/signposts ____.

Other Comments:

Outline Grade: ____

EFFECTIVE SPEAKING IMPROVEMENT WORKSHEET
OPEN-ENDED COMMENT VERSION

Name of speaker: _____ Topic: _____

Comment on these questions: **Suggestions:**

Were you interested in the speaker's **topic**
and why or why not?

What did the speaker do to **open** with impact?
Did it get your attention?

How were you able to identify the speaker's **thesis**?
Write what you think the thesis statement was.

How did the speaker **connect** with the audience?

How did the speaker **preview** the main points of the
speech, and was it clear?

What were the **main points** of the speech?
Were they well-chosen and clearly stated?

How well did the **signposts** indicate that the speaker
was moving from point to point?

What **supporting materials** did the speaker provide for the main points and subpoints of the speech, and were they adequate?

Comment on the speaker's **visual aids** or on other presentational aids that were used. (Were they adequate and appropriate?)

What examples of imaginative, vivid, and appropriate **language** did you note?

What effect did the speaker's **vocal delivery** have on the speech? (Consider variety, energy, and enthusiasm.)

What effect did the speaker's level of **eye contact** with the audience have on the speech?

What did you notice about the speaker's use of **gesture and posture**? (Consider if they were natural and effective in conveying the message.)

How well did the speaker **summarize** the main points of the speech?

What did the speaker do to **conclude** with impact? Was it effective and memorable?

GROUP PRESENTATION EVALUATION CRITERIA

Date: _____

Names of group members:_____

✔+   excellent
✔   minimum requirements were met
✔-   failed to meet criteria/needs improvement

Balanced?

_____   Group members' participation times were balanced.

_____   Group balanced creative/educational/professional components.

Professional?

_____   Overall presentation demonstrated/conveyed professionalism.

_____   Visual aids were professional.

_____   Additional supporting material demonstrated professionalism.

_____   Individual members' appearances and actions demonstrated professionalism.

Added educational value?

_____   Audience learned something new/innovative.

_____   Audience learned something important.

_____   Audience learned something about effective public speaking.

_____   Group members learned/incorporated something new about the topic.

_____   Group members learned something about or demonstrated their understanding of effective public speaking.

_____   Group members told the audience why they should want to learn about the presentation topic. (The presentation included a clear connect with audience statement.)

Organized?

_____ The presentation was (overall) clearly organized.

_____ Content material was organized.

_____ Individual presentations were organized.

_____ Group members used time appropriately.

_____ Group members used available space appropriately.

_____ Presentation(s) demonstrated group planning and practice.

_____ The components/parts of an effective presentation learned in class were included and used appropriately.

Creative?

_____ Demonstrated creative approaches.

_____ Organized content or delivery in a creative way.

_____ Presentation topic demonstrated/conveyed group creativity.

Demonstrate group cohesiveness?

_____ Group looked like a group and sounded like a group.

_____ Group demonstrated a "we not me" orientation.

_____ Group demonstrated synergistic approaches.

_____ Group appeared to have shared tasks and rewards.

Group demonstrated adequate audience analysis?

_____ The audience seemed interested.

_____ Group demonstrated their ethical responsibilities to the audience.

_____ Content and delivery were appropriate for the communication context.

Ideas well supported?

____ Sources were included for added credibility.

____ Sources were credible and this credibility was established for the audience.

____ Information was consistent among group members.

Outline?

____ Followed the format.

____ Included sufficient level of content for instructor's purposes (as discussed in class).

____ Clearly indicated group members' portions of the overall presentation.

____ Demonstrated professionalism.

INDIVIDUAL GROUP MEMBER COMMENTS: INSTRUCTOR'S EVALUATION

Date: _____

Name: _____

Individual Grade: _____

Final Grade: _____

✔+   **excellent**
✔   **minimum requirements were met**
✔-   **failed to meet criteria/needs improvement**

Suggestions for Improvement

_____ Balanced?

_____ Professional?

_____ Added educational value?

_____ Organized?

_____ Creative?

_____ Demonstrates group cohesiveness?

_____ Demonstrates adequate audience analysis?

_____ Ideas are well supported?

Additional Comments on Overall Delivery:

GROUP PRESENTATION PEER EVALUATION
OPEN-ENDED COMMENT VERSION

Date: _____

Your Name: _____

Group members' names: _____

Was the presentation balanced? In what ways?

Were the group members professional? In what ways? Was the overall presentation professional?

Did this presentation have educational value? What did you learn? Why is this important?

Was the presentation organized? Why do you think so?

Was the group creative? How?

Did the group demonstrate group cohesiveness? How?

Did the group demonstrate adequate audience analysis? Why do you think so?

Were ideas well supported? How?

GROUP PRESENTATION PEER EVALUATION
OPEN-ENDED COMMITTEE VERSION

PART TWO

CHAPTER OUTLINES, GUIDELINES, AND TEST ITEMS

CHAPTER 1
PRINCIPLES AND CONTEXTS

INTRODUCTION AND OUTLINE

Chapter 1 introduces students to the basic principles of communication that will be discussed in greater detail throughout the text. Specifically, the chapter introduces students to the following:

I. Modeling communication
   A. The earliest models of communication depicted human communication as linear and mechanistic, usually showing a sender transmitting an encoded message to a receiver who decoded the message.
   B. Later models depicted communication in more interactive terms, adding concepts such as feedback.
   C. Contemporary transactional models more accurately show the process of communication.
      1. The model depicts communication as a system or a collection of interdependent parts arrayed in such a way that a change in one will effect changes in all others.
      2. The system includes:
         a. the environment;
         b. the number of people communicating;
         c. their backgrounds; and
         d. the content and relational sides of messages.
      3. This model suggests that communication between people is simultaneous and continuous rather than turn-taking.
      4. The model reflects that communication is interdependent rather than independent and is heavily influenced by perception.

II. Communication competence
   A. Communication is a skill that has to be learned.
   B. Communication competence is the ability to consciously decide how to most appropriately convey a particular message. It requires two components:
      1. knowledge of the principles and practices of effective communication; and
      2. a conscious decision about how to most appropriately convey a particular message.
   C. Communication involves at least the six following elements.
      1. **Self-competence** is the confidence a person has in his or her communication skills.
      2. **Interpretive competence** is the ability to decode communication accurately.
      3. **Goal competence** is the ability to establish appropriate and achievable communication goals.
      4. **Role competence** is the ability to choose an appropriate pattern of communication behavior based on the interpretation of communication cues and establishment of communication goals.

5. **Message competence** is the ability to choose appropriate verbal and nonverbal behaviors to complement the role.
6. **Performative competence** is the overall and observable consequence of conscious communication competence.

D. Communication competence requires **active mindfulness,** or the conscious awareness of a communication transaction as it unfolds.
   1. Active mindfulness has three requirements.
      a. **Cognitive flexibility** is the ability to create new mental categories for new experiences.
      b. The second requirement is openness to new information as we communicate.
      c. The third requirement is the ability to look at someone or something from multiple perspectives.
   2. A competent communicator is also mindful of the four most common dimensions of communication.

III. The four most common of dimensions of communication covered in *Dimensions of Communication*
A. **Dyadic communication** is communication between two people.
   1. It is the basic building block for other forms of communication, yet it is unique because the dyad has the following properties.
      a. It is characterized by a single line of communication.
      b. It affords communicators the maximum opportunity to monitor verbal and nonverbal behaviors.
      c. It is potentially more intimate than other communication contexts.
      d. It invites greater accuracy in the interpretation of messages.
   2. Dyadic communication can satisfy a number of interpersonal needs including inclusion, affection, and control.
B. **Small group communication** is communication between three or more people who have a mutually interdependent purpose, who engage in communication transactions with one another, and who identify with the norms of the group. Common small group types include the following:
   1. **Informal groups** are typically social groups.
   2. **Formal groups** are commonly hierarchical and organized around activities and interests.
   3. **Therapeutic groups** assist people in overcoming problems.
   4. **Task-oriented groups** or problem-solving groups exist to complete a task or to solve a problem perceived to be beyond the talents and abilities of a single person working alone.
C. Public speaking involves a formal presentation before an audience.
   1. Forty percent of all adults report that public speaking is their number one fear.
   2. Overcoming public speaking anxiety is discussed in detail in Chapter 15.
   3. A speech may serve to entertain, inform, motivate, or persuade an audience.
D. **Mass communication** is communication directed at large audiences through such media as newspapers, magazines, radio, film, and television.
   1. Traditionally, this is a one-to-many system of communication which is inherently slow at responding to audience feedback.

2. In contrast, new media such as the Internet and electronic mail were designed from their inception to compensate for the inherent weaknesses of traditional mass communication systems.

TEACHING/LEARNING OBJECTIVES

After reading Chapter 1, students should:

- Recognize the practical value of increasing their communication skills.

- Understand the transactional model of communication.

- Understand what it means to have communication competence.

- Set personal goals for improving their communication competence.

- Commit to practicing skills taught in *Dimensions of Communication* both in and out of class.

- Meet the learning objectives listed on page 3 in the text.

TROUBLESHOOTING

In Chapter 2 of *Dimensions of Communication*, Scott and Brydon discuss the adage "you never have a second chance to make a first impression." However, instructors need to have this idea in mind before they first step into their classrooms. In addition to introducing basic principles and concepts of communication covered in Chapter 1, you must establish yourself as a role model for communication competence and create an effective classroom climate. Throughout *Dimensions of Communication*, the authors provide students with valuable skills on how to become more communicatively competent. Throughout this instructor's manual, exercises are provided to give students the opportunity to practice these skills. Often, these instructional exercises require appropriate levels of self-disclosure and role-playing, both activities that might initially seem uncomfortable for some students. The classroom environment needs to be psychologically safe, and engaging in class activities should begin as early in the semester or quarter as possible in order to make them routine. When students express their initial embarrassment, remind them that if they can practice with past or pretend scenarios, or share with a stranger, they will feel less embarrassed when it's time for the real thing.

INSTRUCTIONAL EXERCISES

1. Break students into groups of three or four. Have each student take a turn giving a 2–3-minute speech (while standing), with their group members serving as the audience. The topic of the speech should be "The last time I gave a speech" or "The last time I had to work in a small group." Students should briefly recount their experience. Encourage students to use this experience as a catharsis (or as an opportunity to begin a semester or quarter of appropriate self-disclosure). After everyone has had a turn, pull the class back together as one large group. Find out if most people's previous experiences had been successful or unpleasant and what they believe to be the reasons. Use this discussion as an opportunity to discuss what the semester or quarter is going to be like in your class and your goals for making this class a pleasant and beneficial experience for all.

2. Ask students to think of a person that they believe to be a competent communicator. This person must be someone that they interact with frequently, preferably on a daily basis. Ask students to observe this person's behavior and to be prepared, for the next class period, to share specific examples that demonstrate this person's communication competence. Ask the class for their findings and make a master list of competent communication behaviors on the board. Discuss what makes each of these behaviors noticeably effective.

3. Break students into groups of four or five. Provide one student with an 8-1/2 x 11 copy of a series of geometric shapes (for their eyes only). Ask the student to tell members of their group how to draw an identical set of geometric shapes on a piece of notebook paper without using any gestures, facial expressions, vocal variations, or any other form of nonverbal communication. The students who are drawing are not allowed to ask questions or provide any verbal or nonverbal feedback to each other or the student instructing them. They are to work individually and not show their drawing to anyone until the exercise has been completed. Afterward, compare student drawings to the original and lead a discussion on the importance of verbal and nonverbal communication in both initiating and responding to a message. Furthermore, determine how the students provided instructions. Did they describe in terms of north and south, right and obtuse angles, rectangles or isosceles triangles? Use their instructions to discuss the importance of the communicators' backgrounds. Ask students why they were successful or not, and relate their observations to the transactional model of communication and its interdependent parts.

JOURNAL WRITING

Scott and Brydon point out in the text that public speaking is the number one fear of 40% of adults. Therefore, it is likely that you may experience some anxiety about delivering public speeches. Do you feel anxiety about taking this course for the above or any other reason? Consider your anxieties and try to understand their source. Clearly list your anxieties/fears relating this class. Following, list the worst possible thing that could happen and the best possible thing that could happen for each one.

DISCUSSION TOPICS

Ask students why they are taking this class. If this class is a general education requirement, ask why some believe it is important enough to be deemed so. Engage students in a discussion that relates public speaking skills to their future career plans.

Discuss the difference between a linear and transactional model of communication. What are the implications of each for a public speaker? If communication is a transaction, what does this say about the need to understand your audience's needs and purposes? What does this suggest about the importance of eye contact to reading feedback from your audience?

Using the transactional model of communication, discuss the simultaneous roles of senders and receivers. What should senders and receivers do, and what behaviors should they avoid? Then, engage the class in a brainstorming session to determine potential things that could interfere with the message transmission (e.g., poor lighting or internal and external noises).

TEST QUESTIONS

Multiple Choice

1. The earliest communication models depicted communication as all of the following EXCEPT
   a. linear and mechanistic.
   *b. interactive.
   c. a process that showed a sender transmitting an encoded message to a decoder.
   d. none of the above
   Page 5

2. The transactional communication model differs from early models in that it depicts communication as
   a. a process in which a sender transmits an encoded message to a receiver or decoder.
   *b. a system.
   c. a process characterized by turn-taking.
   d. immune to the process of perception.
   Page 5

3. The transactional model suggests that
   a. the environment influences the communication.
   b. communication is simultaneous and continuous rather than a process of turn-taking.
   c. messages have both a content and relationship dimension.
   *d. all of the above
   Page 5

4. The idea that communication is a system basically suggests that
   a. it is a collection of interdependent parts.
   b. a change in one part will affect all the other parts.
   *c. a and b
   d. none of the above
   Page 5

5. Communication is influenced by which of the following factors?
   a. the context in which the communication takes place
   b. the backgrounds of those involved in the transaction
   c. the number of people involved in the transaction
   *d. all of the above
   Page 6

6. An important part of communication competence is
   *a. knowledge of the principles and practices of effective communication.
   b. an unconscious ability to appropriately convey your message.
   c. a large vocabulary.
   d. a pleasant speaking voice.
   Page 10

7. To be consciously competent requires which of the following?
   a. self-competence
   b. interpretive competence
   c. performative competence
   *d. none of the above
   Page 10

8. Interpretive competence is best defined as
   a. the confidence a person has in his or her decoding skills.
   *b. the ability to decode communication accurately.
   c. the ability to choose an appropriate part to play in a specific communication situation.
   d. the ability to choose appropriate verbal and nonverbal behaviors to complement the role.
   Page 11

9. The overall and observable consequence of conscious communication competence is referred to as
   a. goal competence.
   b. message competence.
   *c. performative competence.
   d. self-competence.
   Page 13

10. Active mindfulness is
    a. considering the future outcomes or consequences of sending a particular message.
    *b. focusing on the moment.
    c. the ability to break apart the communication model and examine each part individually to see its effect on the overall transaction.
    d. none of the above
    Page 13

11. The ability to create new mental categories for new experiences rather than trying to force them into old ones is defined as
    a. performative competence.
    *b. cognitive flexibility.
    c. active mindfulness.
    d. interpretive competence.
    Page 13

12. Active mindfulness requires which characteristic(s)?
    a. cognitive flexibility
    b. openness to new information
    c. the ability to look at someone or something from multiple perspectives
    *d. all of the above
    Page 13

13. According to the authors of your text, the most common dimensions of communication are
    *a. dyadic, small group, public, and mass communication.
    b. interpersonal, organizational, and mass communication.
    c. dyadic and small group communication.
    d. dyadic, small group, and mass communication.
    Page 13

14. Dyadic communication explains communication
    *a. between two people.
    b. between three or more people.
    c. in which one person is both the sender and the receiver, such as in intrapersonal communication.
    d. across cultures.
    Page 15

15. Which of the following is a small group relevant to interpersonal communication studies?
    a. therapeutic groups
    b. task-oriented groups
    c. self-help groups
    *d. all of the above
    Page 16

16. Small group communication involves
    a. two or more people.
    b. a one-to-many interaction.
    *c. mutually interdependent purposes.
    d. all of the above
    Page 16

17. Public speaking ranks as the number one fear of what percent of adults?
    a. less than 10%
    b. approximately 25%
    *c. approximately 40%
    d. 90%
    Page 17

18. A speech may serve which of the following purposes?
    a. to motivate
    b. to entertain
    c. to inform
    *d. all of the above
    Page 18

19. According to the authors of your text, a major drawback of mass communication is
    a. the slow process of responding to audience feedback.
    *b. the difficulty of having one message appeal to diverse audiences.
    c. not being able to keep up with advancing technology and electronic communication developments.
    d. all of the above
    Page 18

20. Mass communication includes all of the following EXCEPT
    a. print media.
    *b. delivering a speech in your class.
    c. films.
    d. television shows.
    Page 18

True/False

21. Messages can be either verbal or nonverbal. (True, p. 5)

22. The movie *Stand by Me* demonstrates the idea that as more people are engaged in the communication the topics discussed become less superficial. (False, p. 6)

23. We are sources and receivers simultaneously and continuously. (True, p. 8)

24. The transactional model treats communication as a system of interdependent parts, meaning they have a reciprocal influence on one another. (True, p. 8)

25. Communication is a skill that can be learned. (True, p. 10)

26. Whereas there is only one line between two people communicating, the number of lines increases to nine when three people communicate. (False, p. 16)

Short Answer/Essay

27. Define *perception* and briefly explain its role in communication. (p. 8)

28. Define *communication competence* and the six elements it requires. (p. 10)

29. Explain why the authors of your text believe that "people who communicate inappropriately in real space and time probably will do likewise in their virtual realities." (p. 18)

30. List and explain some steps that you can take to increase your communication competence.

CHAPTER 2
THE ROLE OF PERCEPTION

INTRODUCTION AND OUTLINE

Chapter 2 explains the selective process of perception and how what we see, or fail to see, affects our communication. Specifically, the chapter covers:

I. The anatomy of perception
   A. Perception is the process by which people give meaning to what they sense and experience.
      1. People, places, and things are sensed through sight, sound, smell, taste, and touch.
      2. There is a discrepancy between the capacity of the senses and the capacity of the brain. The eye is capable of sensing much more than the brain is capable of processing.
   B. Selective perception is the predisposition to give meaning to a limited number of sensations and experiences.
      1. Three consequences of this tendency are:
         a. **selective exposure**—the choice to experience or avoid particular stimuli
         b. **selective attention**—the decision whether to be mindful in an encounter
         c. **selective recall**—the ability of people to remember
      2. Factors that influence people's selective perception include the following:
         a. The **background** in which a stimulus is embedded can either facilitate or impede perception and communication.
         b. **Intensity** involves how loud, bright, or vivid a stimulus appears. Generally, the greater the intensity the more likely people will perceive the stimulus.
         c. **Extensity** involves the attention-drawing effect of size.
         d. **Concreteness** involves giving body and definition to complexity so that the stimulus is more readily sensed and grasped.
         e. **Contrast and velocity** affect the degree to which messages and people appear striking, novel, changing, or moving to provoke and sustain selective attention.
         f. **Impressivity** involves using the above five factors in varying combinations to "impress" the senses to take note.
II. Perceiving self
   A. Self-perception involves how we see ourselves. It defines who we are and shapes our communication toward others.
   B. There are at least three parts to self-perception: the ideal, personal, and social self.
      1. The **ideal self** is the idealized version of the person we would like to become.
      2. The **personal self** involves how we see ourselves.
      3. The **social self** involves how we see ourelves based on the way we perceive others see us.

a. Charles Cooley pointed out people engage in **reflected appraisals** or assessments of themselves based on other people's responses toward them.

b. Reflected appraisals lead people to judge themselves in terms of how communicatively skilled they are, how sociable they are, and the extent to which others perceive them as attractive.

III. Perceiving others

A. Attribution is the process of giving reasons to behavior.

B. Social psychologist Fritz Heider asserts the process of attribution involves three stages: (1) perceiving an action; (2) assigning a reason to the action; (3) connecting the reason to the person who engaged in the action.

C. Attributions can be stable or unstable and internal or external.

D. Overcoming attributional bias involves understanding the source.

1. **Centrism** refers to people who believe they are superior to others and leads to attributional bias.

2. **Xenophobia** is the fear of anything strange or foreign, including people, and leads to attributional bias.

3. Increased **emotional intensity** of one's beliefs and feelings may lead to favorable or unfavorable attributional bias.

4. **Overconfidence,** or people's convictions that their interpretation of communication behavior is seldom wrong, leads to attributional bias.

5. Perceived legitimate or illegitimate **power** may lead to attributional bias.

IV. Perceiving yourself and others accurately are learned skills.

A. Making accurate attributions requires engaging in and avoiding certain behaviors.

1. We need to have sufficient evidence to support attributions about ourselves and others.

2. Avoid **fundamental attribution error,** or the tendency to believe that other people's behavior is the result of internal characteristics rather than external factors. To overcome fundamental attribution error, employ at least three skills:

a. Look for signs of covariation. **Covariation** demands the suspension of such definitive attributions until multiple exposures in different communication environments have occurred.

b. Practice discounting. **Discounting** asks people to look beyond the obvious for alternative explanations.

c. Practice **reality checking** with another source.

3. Practice perspective taking and reframing.

a. **Empathy** involves the ability to perceive things from another person's perspective. It is also a nonjudgmental process.

b. **Reframing** is using more than a single view in assessing an experience to change one's point of view.

4. Practice coordinating meaning, which requires that all people involved understand the rules that govern the meaning of their communication transactions.

TEACHING/LEARNING OBJECTIVES

After reading Chapter 2, your students should:

- Respect the role that perception plays in facilitating communication competence.

- Understand the relationship between one's perception and communication.

- Recognize their own likeliness to engage in selective perception.

- Reflect on their individual self-perception and its impact on themselves and their relationships.

- Practice using the tools described in Chapter 2 to enhance selective perception.

- Understand the roots of attributional bias in an effort to avoid being subject to it in future communication transactions.

- Commit to a continual effort to improve perceiving oneself and others more accurately.

- Meet the learning objectives listed on page 23 in the text.

INSTRUCTIONAL EXERCISES

1. On three-inch pieces of masking tape, write the names of professions and/or personal characteristics. Place one piece of tape on each student's forehead without allowing them to see "who they are." Have students walk around and interact with other classmates. They are to communicate with each other in a way that reflects the labels they see on others. Based on these interactions, students are to ask "Am I _____?" Periodically check with the class to see if everyone has determined their identity. Engage the class in a discussion regarding how self-perceptions are created. Possible labels include a pessimist, an optimist, a private investigator, a teacher, a religious leader, or a child.

2. Competent communicators aim to make accurate attributions about themselves and others. In order to do this, people must first understand the sources of attributional bias and avoid fundamental attribution error. To provide students with valuable practice at lessening attributional bias, break them into groups of four. Each student must reflect on a behavior that he or she engages in now or in the past that hinders effective communication. In fact, this behavior can be real or fictional to save embarrassment. Each student is to take turns sharing this behavior with the group and offering an attribution. Using Chapter 2 as a guide, each additional member of the group is to offer one potential reason or source for this behavior. Students are to ask questions regarding the behavior that encourage (1) looking for signs of covariation, (2) discounting, and (3) reality checking before they offer their attribution.

JOURNAL WRITING

In Chapter 2, we learn how our self-perception is developed and the role it plays on how we communicate with others. Scott and Brydon explain that self-perception comprises the ideal, personal, and social self. Take some time to reflect on your own self-perception. What is your ideal self? Has this goal changed? When? Why? Reflect on how you really see yourself. Do you like what you see? Why? Why not? Finally, consider your social self on two counts. Does your social self seem to closely reflect your ideal self? And how do the relationships that you choose to develop and maintain influence your individual self-perception? Be specific.

DISCUSSION TOPICS

Discuss who students in the class perceive to be as credible individuals in both the public and private spheres. For example, how credible do they view local newscasters, business owners, and political figures to be?

Engage the class in a discussion that helps students to distinguish between legitimate and illegitimate power. Ask them to consider situations where they find themselves influenced by the perception of power in their daily experiences. Through discussion determine if the power is legitimate or not by returning to the question posed by Scott and Brydon, "Does the other person perceive that he or she has any choice in the matter?" You may want to begin with your position as the college instructor and the power that it holds.

Engage the class in a discussion which explores the question as to whether or not people from a different culture perceive and communicate differently. Ask students to provide reasons for their belief. Use this question and discussion to lead into information presented in Chapter 3 which addresses the relationship between communication and language.

TEST QUESTIONS

Multiple Choice

1. Perception can best be defined as
    a. the process that initiates people's recall of past experiences.
    *b. the process by which people give meaning to what they sense and experience.
    c. being predisposed to give meaning to sensory data that are familiar and especially intense.
    d. a conscious decision as to whether or not to be completely mindful to an event in an effort to expand one's repertoire of experiences.
    Page: 24

2. The meaning people give to what they sense depends on
    a. direct experiences.
    b. vicarious experiences.
    c. their ability to see, hear, smell, taste, and touch.
    *d. all of the above
    Page: 25

3. The idea that people are predisposed to give meaning to sensory data that are familiar is best defined as
   a. perception.
   b. selective attention.
   c. selective recall.
   *d. selective perception.
   Page: 25

4. Selective attention is all of the following EXCEPT
   a. voluntary.
   b. the decision whether to be mindful in an encounter.
   c. potentially manipulated by the communicator.
   *d. none of the above
   Page: 26

5. Research indicates which of the following factors frequently influence people's selective perception?
   *a. background, intensity, extensity, concreteness, contrast and velocity, and impressivity
   b. culture, language, contrast, vividness, impressivity
   c. culture, magnitude, contrast
   d. language, mindfulness, intensity, size, context
   Page: 26

6. Using a scale model helps to increase selective perceptions by appealing to the need for
   a. impressivity.
   b. contrast.
   *c. concreteness.
   d. none of the above
   Page: 27

7. Self-perception involves all of the following EXCEPT
   a. how you see yourself.
   b. how you communicate with others.
   *c. the projected, personal, and professional self.
   d. b and c
   Page: 30

8. Philosophers and social scientists have identified what three parts to self-perception?
   *a. ideal, personal, and social
   b. projected, personal, and professional
   c. perfect, personal, and professional
   d. ideal, professional, and social
   Page: 30

9. The personal self refers to all of the following EXCEPT
   *a. the way you interact in your interpersonal relationships.
   b. the way you really see yourself.
   c. the way you see yourself, sometimes based on how others in your interpersonal relationships behave toward you.
   d. a subjective self-perception.
   Page: 30

10. The idea of reflected appraisals was originated by
    a. Fritz Heider.
    *b. Charles Cooley.
    c. George Orwell.
    d. William Rawlins.
    Page: 32

11. Reflected appraisals suggest that people judge themselves on which grounds?
    a. how communicatively skilled they are
    b. how sociable they are
    c. the extent to which other people find them attractive
    *d. all of the above
    Page: 32

12. Attribution refers to
    a. giving credit where credit is due.
    *b. giving reasons to behavior.
    c. accepting individual responsibility for creating one's self perception.
    d. acknowledging selective perception.
    Page: 32

13. The process of attribution involves which stages?
    a. (1) assigning meaning to an action; (2) connecting the reason to the person who engaged in the action; (3) assigning value to the action and reason
    b. (1) perceiving an action; (2) assigning a reason to the action; (3) connecting the reason to the person who engaged in the action; (4) assigning value to the action and reason
    *c. (1) perceiving an action; (2) assigning a reason to the action; (3) connecting the reason to the person who engaged in the action
    d. none of the above
    Page: 32

14. Attribution can be
    a. directed at oneself or at another person.
    b. stable or unstable.
    c. external or internal.
    *d. all of the above
    Page: 33

15. According to research by Alan Sillars,
    *a. attributions people make about themselves tend to be either generous or forgiving whereas attributions directed toward others tend to be more fault-finding.
    b. attributions people make about themselves tend to be more fault-finding and judgmental than the more forgiving and generous attributions bestowed onto others.
    c. attributions are subjective and therefore cannot be generalized about.
    d. none of the above
    Page: 33

16. Centrism refers to
    a. providing reasons for another person's behavior.
    *b. people's belief that they are superior to others.
    c. the fear of anything unfamiliar.
    d. considering how other people see you in order to alter your self-perception.
    Page: 34

17. Which statement about power is accurate?
    a. Power can be derived from skills and the ability to reward others.
    b. Power stems from others desiring to be identified with the person perceived as powerful.
    c. Power can be legitimate or illegitimate, known or unknown.
    *d. all of the above
    Page: 36

18. Fundamental attribution error
    a. occurs when one shifts perspective to change one's point of view based on a single piece of evidence.
    b. occurs when one fails to assess the accuracy of perceptions with another source.
    *c. occurs when people believe that other people's behavior is the result of internal characteristics rather than external circumstances.
    d. occurs when one wrongly shifts their perspective to match other people's points of view.
    Page: 37

19. Discounting refers to
    *a. asking people to look beyond the obvious for alternative explanations.
    b. failing to look beyond the obvious to search for alternative explanations.
    c. failing to accept the obvious reasons and searching for alternative explanations.
    d. none of the above
    Page: 38

20. The ability to perceive things from another person's perspective is
    a. one of the earliest signs of moving into adolescence.
    *b. best known as empathy.
    c. also referred to as reframing.
    d. a sign of a weak self-image.
    Page: 38

21. Using more than a single view in assessing an experience is called
   a. empathy.
   b. perception competence.
   *c. reframing.
   d. all of the above
   Page: 39

True/False

22. Research indicates that the brain is capable of processing much more data than the eye actually captures. (False, p. 25)

23. People are predisposed to assign meaning to sensory data that is unfamiliar because of our uncomfortableness with the unknown. (False, p. 25)

24. Research indicates that language that is moderately intense—only slightly at odds with people's expectations versus shocking—is more attention-getting and involving. (True, p. 27)

25. According to social psychologist Charles Cooley, the process of attribution involves three stages. (False, p. 32)

26. The fear of foreign people is called centrism. (False, p. 34)

27. The fear of foreign people is called xenophobia. (True, p. 34)

Short Answer/Essay

28. Define and explain the differences and similarities between perception, selective perception, selective exposure, selective attention, and selective recall. (pp. 24–26)

29. List and explain the six specific factors that frequently influence people's selective perception. Provide specific examples. (p. 26)

30. Explain the relationship between how we see ourselves and how we see others. (p. 32)

31. Researchers have uncovered a number of sources of attributional bias about which we should be mindful. List and explain at least five. (p. 34)

32. Explain the difference between empathy and sympathy. (p. 38)

CHAPTER 3
COMMUNICATION AND LANGUAGE

INTRODUCTION AND OUTLINE

Chapter 3 thoroughly explains the concept that language is not neutral. Students learn that the language they use to speak and think influences their perceptions of themselves, others, and reality. In this chapter, effective language is distinguished from language that promotes communication breakdown. Specifically, Chapter 3 covers:

I. Language: The relationship between words and things
   A. Words influence what we perceive; what we perceive influences our attitudes and communication behavior toward the person, place, or thing the word describes.
   B. The language in which we think and speaks affects how we perceive our world and the people in it.
      1. The **linguistic relativity hypothesis,** developed by cultural anthropologist Benjamin Whorf, suggests that different languages lead to different patterns of thought.
      2. In addition to influencing perception, the language we speak and in which we think can restrict our ability to see the reality perceived by people from different cultures who speak a different language.
   C. The structure of language, which involves words, grammar, and syntax, influences perceptions.
      1. Words have different uses including standard, informal, obsolete, and slang.
      2. Words have different meanings.
         a. **Denotative meaning** refers to the dictionary definition of a word.
         b. **Connotative meaning** is the ideas associated with a word, often containing an emotional element.
      3. Words are put together following rules.
         a. Grammar is a system of rules governing the way words are formed and combined.
         b. Syntax is a system of rules governing the order of words.

II. Language and the three levels of diversity (cultural, group, and individual)
   A. To understand a people's culture, it is necessary to understand their language.
      1. Keep in mind that not everyone who shares a language has the same culture (e.g., Spanish-speaking people in Spain, Mexico, Los Angeles, and Florida).
      2. The degree to which spoken language influences how people think, feel, and behave also depends on whether they live in a high- or low-context culture.
         a. In high-context cultures, people infer much about the meaning of their communication transaction from the environment in which it occurs.
         b. In low-context cultures, people invest considerable meaning in what they say to each other and make no distinction based on the environment in which it takes place.

B. Language affects all reference groups but especially gender, social class, and race.
   1. Gender roles and their expectancies are partly shaped by the language members of a specific culture use when talking about gender.
   2. The way classes are shaped and the social class in which you consider yourself are results of the way a culture uses language.
   3. Race is influenced by language, however, often negatively as in the case of stereotyping.
   4. People within reference groups use language to create convergence or divergence.
      a. **Convergence** is the use of language to create a reference group and to define its members as highly similar.
      b. **Divergence** is the use of language to exclude people from a reference group.
C. How people perceive themselves and others is tied to language.
   1. Individual diversity is reflected in people's personal viewpoints.
   2. Recognizing individual diversity does not mean you always have to agree but rather you should take such viewpoints into account when communicating.
   3. To learn about people's viewpoints, ask appropriate questions and listen to their words and how they use them.

III. The relationship between language and power
   A. Language can communicate power or powerlessness.
      1. Powerful people use competence-enhancing language.
         a. This kind of language is appropriately direct and may contain words and phrases that document with evidence the importance of what is being said.
         b. People who use powerful language are perceived as more credible, attractive, and competent than people who use powerless language.
      2. Powerless language contains:
         a. **Verbal qualifiers**—tentative words and phrases that diminish the power of language
         b. **Verbal intensifiers**—words that undermine perceptions of power as a result of overemphasis
         c. **Tag questions**—declarative statements turned into questions to solicit approval
   B. Language can marginalize.
      1. Marginalizing language involves words and phrases that disenfranchise individuals and specific groups of people.
      2. When a group of people are consistently described in marginal terms, it affects both how the group is viewed by others and how the group views itself.
      3. People on the margins of power also tend to be the preferred targets of those who use hate speech.
   C. Ambiguous language can cause communication breakdowns.
      1. The term *communication breakdown* refers to an exchange between people that wasn't understood as intended.
      2. Three common sources of ambiguous language are relative terms, abstract words, and euphemisms.

IV. Effective language has at least the following five characteristics.
   A. Inclusive language—words and phrases that assist people in believing they have a stake in and power regarding matters of social importance.
   B. Language that is appropriate rather than simply correct.
   C. Uncertainty-reducing language—words and phrases that make messages more specific and less ambiguous.
   D. Immediate language—words and phrases that increase the perception of psychological closeness between communicators.
   E. Language that is responsive to varying learning styles.

TEACHING/LEARNING OBJECTIVES

After reading Chapter 3, students should:

- Feel confident that in order to be a consciously competent communicator one must understand the complex relationship between communication and language.

- Understand the essence of the statement "language is not neutral."

- Recognize the importance of the relationship between language and diversity.

- Distinguish between powerful and powerless language in their own communication and the communication of others.

- Practice avoiding powerless language.

- Commit to continual efforts to practice effective language.

- Meet the learning objectives listed on page 45 in the text.

TROUBLESHOOTING

In Chapter 3, Scott and Brydon discuss the different ways people learn: by seeing, hearing, and doing. Furthermore, they suggest that to maximize listeners' receptivity to what is said, people must make every effort to use words that reflect different styles of information processing. One thing that instructors might want to keep in mind when teaching is that they are becoming models of competent communicators for their students. As a result, when they are given specific *dos* and *dont's*, such as those mentioned above, or the list of five ways to effectively use language, students are likely to use these new tools to measure your teaching effectiveness.

INSTRUCTIONAL EXERCISES

1. Communication breakdown can be a common occurrence with family members, roommates, significant others, and friends. Communication breakdown becomes a potential threat to the relationship only when those involved do not initiate further communication to clarify the original intent of the message that was misinterpreted. This exercise aims to provide students with practice at the invaluable skill of initiating that conversation and seeking clarification. It also provides students with an opportunity to relive past communication breakdowns, this time with a happy ending.

Break students into groups of two. Give students about five minutes to discuss personal experiences of communication breakdowns. Each student should contribute one experience to be role-played. In this role-playing scenario, the person who "owns" the scenario should play the role opposite himself or herself in the initial encounter. The partner should play the part of the person the original situation happened to. The partner should misinterpret the original message but initiate a conversation that aims to rebuild what broke down. Change scenarios and switch roles.

2. Ask students to write down the cultural and reference groups with which they identify themselves. Then, ask them to write down some attitudes, beliefs, and values that make them individually diverse. After everyone has completed their lists, about 3–4 minutes, ask the class to share their lists while you write their additions on the board to gain the visual effect of the vast diversity in a single classroom. Engage the class in a discussion regarding this diversity, and ask students to consider how this might affect the way that they construct and deliver a speech in class.

    Following, ask them to imagine how much diversity must be in the university community, local community, state, and so on. Based on the potential diversity you reveal in your communities, ask students to brainstorm how this might affect their day-to-day interactions.

3. Develop a list of ambiguous words that may lead to communication breakdown. They may be relative terms, abstract words, or euphemisms, but they should be commonly used. List these words on the board. Ask students to come up with a substitute word(s) that would be more accurate and therefore less likely to promote communication breakdown.

JOURNAL WRITING

Recall a recent experience in which you interacted with a person who was culturally or socially diverse. For what reason were you interacting? To what degree were you successful at recognizing the diversity? Was the interaction successful overall? Why? Why not? What should you have done differently? If it is difficult for you to recall an experience, use this time to set some personal goals to increase your opportunities to communicate with people from diverse backgrounds. Be specific.

DISCUSSION TOPICS

Engage the class in a discussion regarding sites on the Internet where they found hate speech, marginalizing or biased language, or other topics they found to be inappropriate. Lead a class in a discussion as to how to balance rights to freedom of expression with what they have learned about in Chapter 3 regarding the power of language on perceptions.

In Chapter 3, we learn about the linguistic relativity hypothesis. Capitalizing on the cultural diversity in the classroom, ask students to share words from their native tongue that have no translations to English.

TEST QUESTIONS

Multiple Choice

1. Words can be described as all of the following EXCEPT
   a. influencing perception.
   *b. neutral.
   c. descriptive.
   d. powerful.
   Page: 45

2. Language is best defined as
   a. word choices which slant perceptions.
   b. the use of words to create meaning.
   *c. an arbitrary system of symbols used for communicating.
   d. a word system used to communicate both denotative and connotative meanings.
   Page: 46

3. The idea that different languages can lead to different patterns of thought originated with
   a. Carol Gilligan.
   b. Aristotle.
   *c. Benjamin Whorf.
   d. Edward T. Hall.
   Page: 48

4. The linguistic relativity hypothesis suggests that
   *a. the language one speaks influences thinking.
   b. denotative and connotative meanings of words will vary from culture to culture.
   c. language is not neutral but is determined by the context in which it is communicated.
   d. the word is an arbitrary symbol.
   Page: 48

5. All of the following are ways to categorize vocabulary words EXCEPT
   a. obsolete.
   b. informal.
   c. slang.
   *d. syntactical.
   Page: 49

6. _____ is the dictionary definition of a word whereas _____ involves a more personal meaning.
   *a. Denotative; connotative
   b. Connotative; denotative
   Page: 50

7. Connotative meaning is accurately described by all of the following EXCEPT
   a. a meaning that is not typically found in the dictionary.
   *b. a meaning that is found in the dictionary.
   c. a meaning largely determined by cultural usage.
   d. a meaning learned over a period of time.
   Page: 50

8. _____ refers to the objective, conventional meaning of a word.
   a. Connotation
   b. Syntax
   *c. Denotation
   d. Divergence
   Page: 50

9. Grammar can best be defined as
   a. a system of rules of language governing the order of words to form phrases, clauses, and sentences.
   *b. a system of rules of language governing the way words are formed and combined.
   c. an arbitrary system of organizing symbols for the purpose of communicating orally or in writing.
   d. none of the above
   Page: 50

10. Which of the following are the three dimensions of diversity?
    a. cultural, societal, and group
    *b. cultural, group, and individual
    c. societal, individual, and psychological
    d. cultural, ethnic, and individual
    Page: 50

11. When considering group diversity, which of the following are appropriate subjects?
    a. fraternities and sororities
    b. professional work groups
    c. political affiliation groups
    *d. all of the above
    Page: 52

12. When considering group diversity, which of the following are relevant?
    a. gender
    b. ethnicity
    c. social class
    *d. all of the above
    Page: 52

13. All of the following are true statements about gender EXCEPT that
    a. it includes roles people are expected to perform.
    *b. it is the same as biological sex.
    c. it affects one's self-concept.
    d. it affects conversational styles.
    Page: 52

14. Communication scholar _____ argues that language not only constructs an image of race but also is used to justify racism.
    a. Edward T. Hall
    *b. Cheris Kramarae
    c. Carol Gilligan
    d. none of the above
    Page: 54

15. The use of language to create a reference group and to define its members as highly similar is known as
    a. divergence.
    b. immediate language.
    *c. convergence.
    d. dyadic negotiation.
    Page: 54

16. The use of language to exclude members from a reference group is best known as _____ ; language aiming to demonstrate similarity among members is known as _____ .
    a. convergence; divergence
    *b. divergence; convergence
    Page: 54

17. Powerless language is most likely to contain which of the following?
    a. totalizing language
    *b. tag questions
    c. relative terms
    d. marginalizing language
    Page: 56

18. The statement "I'm giving this project to you because I am counting on you to come through for me. This is a very, very important task" is an example of
    a. a verbal qualifier.
    *b. a verbal intensifier.
    c. marginalizing language.
    d. inclusive language.
    Page: 56

19. Tag questions are
    a. declarative sentences turned into questions to solicit approval.
    b. a form of powerless language.
    c. not always considered weak.
    *d. all of the above
    Page: 56

20. "Words and phrases that disenfranchise individuals and specific groups of people" is a definition of
    a. divergence.
    *b. marginalizing language.
    c. convergence.
    d. verbal qualifiers.
    Page: 57

21. According to the authors of your text, the intent of users of hate language is to
    a. anger those who are the subject of the message.
    *b. strip their targets of their humanity and self-worth.
    c. gain support for their message.
    d. bring attention to the speakers and their views.
    Page: 60

22. Words that need a point of comparison in order to be understood are called
    a. abstract words.
    *b. relative terms.
    c. euphemisms.
    d. verbal qualifiers.
    Page: 60

23. Referring to someone as "petite" instead of "short" is
    a. a verbal intensifier.
    b. a verbal qualifier.
    *c. a euphemism.
    d. a relative term.
    Page: 61

24. Effective language is
    a. inclusive.
    b. uncertainty reducing.
    *c. both of the above
    d. neither of the above
    Page: 62

25. Words and phrases that assist people in believing they have a stake in and power regarding matters of societal importance describes
    a. uncertainty-reducing language.
    *b. inclusive language.
    c. immediate language.
    d. none of the above
    Page: 62

True/False

26. Language is neutral. (False, p. 45)

27. On the average, college students have vocabularies between 50,000 and 75,000 words. (False, p. 49)

28. The United States is an example of a high-context culture. (False, p. 52)

29. Recognizing diversity means that we must agree with every viewpoint a person from another culture, with which we are unfamiliar, expresses. (False, p. 55)

30. Trying to adapt to everyone's individual learning styles is an example of powerless language choices. (False, p. 62)

Short Answer/Essay

31. Explain the statement that words influence what we perceive and what we perceive influences how we communicate. (p. 48)

32. Explain the statement "Our native tongue can restrict our ability to see the reality perceived by people from different cultures." Provide specific examples. (p. 49)

33. Explain the differences and similarities between high-context cultures and low-context cultures. (p. 52)

34. List and explain the three common forms of ambiguous language. (p. 60)

35. According to the authors of your text, effective language has at least five characteristics. List and explain these characteristics and provide specific examples. (p. 62)

CHAPTER 4
NONVERBAL COMMUNICATION

INTRODUCTION AND OUTLINE

This chapter is intended to show why people need to be mindful of their own nonverbal communication and of the inferences they make on the basis of the nonverbal communication of others. Specifically, Chapter 4 discusses:

I. Distinguishing characteristics of nonverbal communication
   A. Nonverbal communication is the wordless system of codes that, in combination, convey messages.
   B. Nonverbal communication differs from verbal communication in at least the following four areas:
      1. Nonverbal messages are continuous.
         a. They are unlike verbal messages, which can be divided into separate units such as nouns, verbs, and adjectives.
         b. A smile, which conveys happiness, involves the eyes, brow, and lips and cannot be broken down into its individual parts.
      2. Nonverbal messages are multichanneled.
         a. They are unlike verbal messages, whether spoken or written, which are word driven.
         b. Conveying a message nonverbally requires the message be sent over more than one channel such as auditory or visual.
      3. Nonverbal messages involve the simultaneous use of these channels.
         a. Nonverbal communication is expressed across two or more channels simultaneously.
         b. Returning to the smile example, we do not first raise the corners of our mouth, then change the position of our eyebrows.
      4. Nonverbal communication is spontaneous.
         a. It is unlike verbal communication, which is typically planned communication.
         b. Nonverbal communication occurs at a subconscious level.

II. The nonverbal communication system
   A. The nonverbal system is composed of at least seven interdependent codes of behavior which include appearance; the face and eyes; the voice; the body; touch; space, distance, and territory; and time.
   B. The significance of appearance to communication can be measured in at least two ways.
      1. First impressions are largely based on appearance including body type and height, skin and hair color, and clothing and accessories.
         a. Beauty standards may vary among cultures and beauty is to some degree in the eye of the beholder, yet standards people use to define attractive are very specific.
         b. Research indicates that people perceived as physically attractive are also perceived as smart, successful, sociable, and self-confident.

2. People use criteria to judge not only someone else's physical attractiveness, but also their own. Self-perceptions of physical attractiveness impact one's self-confidence.

C. In North America, people infer a great deal from the face and eyes.
1. Researcher Paul Ekman indicates that the face signals the following eight emotions with a high degree of meaning: happiness, surprise, fear, anger, disgust, contempt, sadness, and interest.
2. Research indicates that the face is rich in nonverbal cues signaling the intensity of the emotion experienced or the degree of control people have over the emotion.
3. Eye behavior, technically called **oculesics,** adds to the potential meaning that can be derived from a facial expression.
4. Although the face and eyes can be rich in meaning, accurate interpretations are more probable when they are considered in conjunction with other nonverbal cues and the content of a person's message.

D. Every person has a unique voice which they are often judged upon.
1. The voice is a significant medium of emotional expression, but unlike the face and eyes, the voice is comparatively easy to manipulate in an attempt to project a certain image.
2. How people use their voice to embellish the content of their messages depends on their interaction goals.

E. The study of movement, or the way people use their bodies to embellish verbal messages, is called **kinesics.**
1. In interpersonal communication, a person's gestures and movements usually are spontaneous and informal, reflecting both the context and content of a message.
2. Table 4-1 lists the common way we use our bodies to communicate and the functions such body movements perform.
   a. **Emblems** translate directly to a few words at most.
   b. **Illustrators** complement verbal behavior and add to its clarity.
   c. **Affect displays** usually add to what the face tells us about an emotion.
   d. **Regulators** control interactions.
   e. **Self-adapters** help people compensate for feelings of anxiety by touching themselves.

F. The study of how people use and respond to touch is called **haptics.**
1. How people use and respond to touch varies according to culture, reference groups, and individual psychologies.
2. Both the initiation of and response to touch depends on where people communicate, the type of relationship between communicators, and knowledge of the normative and situational rules for touching.

G. The study of the ways that space, distance, and territory affect human interaction is called **proxemics.**
1. The configuration of space in an environment can either facilitate or impede communication.
   a. Sociopetal environments stimulate human involvement.
   b. Sociofugal environments make people feel distant.
2. Personal distance norms are a consequence of culture and relationships.
3. Territory is geographically fixed and marked by explicit or implicit signs that are meant to communicate "ownership" of a particular area.

4. The need for personal space, distance, and territory appears to be innate. When denied proxemic satisfaction, people (and their relationships) are likely to suffer.

H. The study of time is called **chronemics.**
   1. There are two types of time: inner and imposed.
   2. Culture imposes time on us, and might be at odds with our inner body clock.

III. Functions of nonverbal communication
   A. According to Professor Dale Leathers, nonverbal messages perform six major functions:
      1. provide information;
      2. regulate interaction;
      3. express emotions;
      4. add meaning through metacommunication (the message about the message);
      5. control behavior; and
      6. facilitate satisfaction of needs.
   B. The degree to which nonverbal communication successfully performs these functions varies with individual skill.

IV. Nonverbal skill development
   A. Not everyone is equally skilled in using or interpreting nonverbal behavior. Typically women are more skilled than men in this regard.
   B. Following are ways to increase skill in using and interpreting nonverbal messages.
      1. Understand common misconceptions about nonverbal communication.
         a. To assign specific meaning to a single nonverbal cue is a mistake. The meaning of a nonverbal cue needs to be considered in relation to other cues, both verbal and nonverbal.
         b. Nonverbal cues are not easily decoded.
            (1) **Quasi-courtship behaviors** are nonverbal behaviors which are frequently mistaken for flirting such as eye contact, primping, touching, and blushing.
            (2) Research suggests that people think they can decode nonverbal cues with greater accuracy than they actually can.
         c. Nonverbal messages are not always superior to verbal messages. When messages contradict one another, it is often problematic to act upon the nonverbal message and your interpretation of it.
         d. To verify meaning of nonverbal messages, engage in **cross-modality checking,** a process in which you check and compare channels of communication.
      2. Recognize the role that diversity plays in nonverbal communication.
         a. Nonverbal communication varies from culture to culture.
         b. To increase success, competent communicators:
            (1) Look for more than the most obvious signs of cultural diversity in making decisions about nonverbal messages and their meaning.
            (2) Consider the specific reference groups with which people identify.
            (3) Consider individual diversity.

3. Learn about self-monitoring.
    a. This technique involves looking for cues about socially appropriate communication behavior and about how people are responding to your communication behavior.
    b. To successfully self-monitor your nonverbal communication, you need to (1) recognize important cues; (2) interpret those cues once you recognize them; (3) analyze the potential consequences of your response; and (4) respond appropriately to those cues.
4. Familiarize yourself with the concept of nonverbal immediacy.
    a. Immediacy involves people's perceptions of how close they are to others.
    b. Immediacy skills promote the perception of closeness.
    c. People who are perceived as immediate sustain eye contact; smile; show signs of attentiveness; directly face the other person; punctuate verbal behavior with facial expressions and illustrative gestures; and stand or sit in appropriately close proximity to the other person.

TEACHING/LEARNING OBJECTIVES

After reading Chapter 4, students should:

- Recognize the important role that nonverbal communication plays in the communication transaction.

- Commit to engaging in self-monitoring behavior in an effort to increase their nonverbal skills.

- Be less likely to assign specific meaning to a single nonverbal cue.

- Abandon common misconceptions about nonverbal communication.

- Plan to incorporate strategies for establishing immediacy in their individual and group presentations.

- Meet the learning objectives listed on page 71 in the text.

TROUBLESHOOTING

In a class where we stress that communication behaviors vary from culture to culture and teach diversity responsive communication, a potential problem arises when we encourage students to engage in immediacy-establishing behaviors. Scott and Brydon suggest that it is beneficial to be perceived as immediate when meeting someone for the first time, interviewing for a job, leading a group, or delivering a speech. They add that nonverbal behaviors which promote immediacy include, sustaining eye contact, smiling, and directly facing the other person.

If you have a multicultural classroom, it is possible that students will resist practicing certain immediacy skills because they conflict with their cultural backgrounds. For example, sustained eye contact is considered rude or a sign of aggression in certain cultures, and as a result some students may be reluctant to practice this skill when delivering a speech or working in a small group. If this conflict arises, it is important to respect the diversity while explaining that many North American audiences respond favorably to these immediacy-establishing behaviors.

INSTRUCTIONAL EXERCISES

1. Engage the classroom in a quick game of charades. The object of the game is to have audience members engaging in the process of cross-modality checking.

    Solicit six volunteers from the audience and divide them into teams of two. Provide them with a message that they are to "communicate" to each other for the audience's review. Instruct students who are "partner one" that they must relay the same message across all channels of communication. However, partner two may choose to be consistent in all messages or choose to cross signals. Inform students who are "partner two" that they must decide before they begin because they will be required to tell the audience their signals and intended meanings later. You may choose to allow student communicators to use verbal and nonverbal messages, or nonverbal only. Audience members are to write down on a sheet of paper what they believe to be the intended message and whether their cross-modality checking indicates consistency or lack thereof and on whose part. After all volunteers have communicated their message, check their results with the student communicators' explanations.

    Possible partner messages include:
    *   Partner one: I really like you.
        Partner two: I like you too (or I think I like you kind of).
    *   Partner one: I'm your supervisor and I'm angry at you.
        Partner two: I'm really sorry (Not!).
    *   Partner one: I saved a lot of my part-time job money to buy you this gift.
        Partner two: I really love it (for my dog).

2. If this exercise was not used in Chapter 1, use it to demonstrate the benefits of nonverbal communication.

    Break students into groups of four or five. Provide one student with an 8-1/2 x 11 copy of a series of geometric shapes (for their eyes only). Ask the student to tell members of their group how to draw an identical set of geometric shapes on a piece of notebook paper without using any gestures, facial expressions, vocal variations, or any other form of nonverbal communication. The students who are drawing are not allowed to ask questions or provide any verbal or nonverbal feedback to each other or the student instructing them. They are to work individually and not show their drawings to anyone until the exercise has been completed. Afterward, compare student drawings to the original and lead a discussion on the importance of nonverbal communication in both initiating and responding to a message.

JOURNAL WRITING

Chapter 4 opens with an experience in which a woman learned a lesson about reading a person based on nonverbal communication. She mistook a young man on a train, who displayed extreme signs of nervousness, as a threat to her young daughter and herself. In reality he was a grandson worried about the grandmother he was separated from. Consider your own daily experiences. Can you recount an instance where you were mistaken in your interpretations of nonverbal cues and were proved wrong? How did you feel when you realized that you were wrong in your assumptions? When assigning meaning to nonverbal cues, are you more likely to consider the best or the worst possible scenario? Why do you think this is so?

At your next opportunity, whether it be at a party, small group meeting, or during a night out with your friends, commit to engaging in self-monitoring behavior. Recount this experience. Be sure to include specifics about the behavior you were engaged in. What cues did you recognize from others? How did you know how to interpret these cues? Or, what led you to act on these interpretations? What choices did you have in terms of responding? Did you consider the potential consequences of your response? What were they? How did you respond? What was the outcome?

DISCUSSION TOPICS

In Box 4-1, Scott and Brydon point out that although men are becoming increasingly body conscious, women have been most affected in this regard. In most cases, students are aware of women's struggle to live up to the media's ideal. In what ways, if any, do men share a similar plight?

Whether it is right or wrong, many people's first impression of you is based on your appearance alone. With this in mind, initiate a discussion regarding appropriate types of attire for men and women in specific contexts. For example, what should students wear to class? On a job interview? To a sports banquet?

Discuss the nonverbal system. Discuss the impacts of the nonverbal codes of behavior on public speakers including appearance; face and eyes; the voice; body; touch; space, distance, and territory; and time. For each of these codes, ask students to provide specific examples of how differences could potentially affect a speaker. For example, what is the difference between speaking at 8 A.M., 11 A.M., and 4 P.M.? What if the room has uncomfortable chairs or is poorly lit? What if the speaker has a cold and a strained voice? Continue along this line and ask for examples of each component of the system and how it might affect a speaker and the audience. Which of these elements are most likely to be under the speaker's control and which are not? For those that are not, how can the speaker adapt?

TEST QUESTIONS

Multiple Choice

1. In the opening paragraph of Chapter 4, we learn that syndicated columnist Diana Griego Erwin
   a. misunderstood the nonverbal cues of an elderly man who in actuality needed help.
   *b. misunderstood the nonverbal messages of a young man who in actuality was separated from his grandmother.
   c. misunderstood the nonverbal messages of her teenage daughter who in actuality was not using drugs.
   d. none of the above
   Page: 72

2. The authors of your text define *nonverbal communication* as
   a. incorporating your overall appearance, facial expressions, eye contact, posture, and gestures to affect how you are perceived by the audience.
   b. all forms of communication other than words themselves.
   *c. a wordless system of codes that, in combination, convey messages.
   d. planned, discrete behavior.
   Page: 72

3. Interpretive communication competence concerns
   *a. the degree to which people accurately assess the communication cues they perceive.
   b. the degree to which people accurately assess nonverbal communication cues they receive.
   c. the accuracy with which one is able to distinguish between the denotative and connotative meanings of language.
   d. the accuracy to which senders and receivers are able to respond appropriately to verbal and nonverbal feedback.
   Page: 72

4. All of the following are characteristics which distinguish verbal from nonverbal communication EXCEPT which of the following?
   a. Nonverbal communication is spontaneous.
   *b. Nonverbal communication is an unconscious response.
   c. Nonverbal messages involve the simultaneous use of multiple channels.
   d. none of the above
   Page: 72

5. Which of the following characteristics distinguishes verbal from nonverbal communication?
   *a. Nonverbal messages are continuous.
   b. Nonverbal messages relay multiple meanings.
   c. Nonverbal behaviors are contagious in the communication transaction.
   d. all of the above
   Page: 72

6. The idea that nonverbal communication is simultaneous suggests that
   a. nonverbal communication complements verbal communication.
   b. nonverbal and verbal messages are simultaneously expressed.
   *c. nonverbal communication is expressed across two or more channels to convey meaning.
   d. nonverbal communication can occur only during verbal communication.
   Page: 73

7. The following nonverbal messages typically originate at the subconscious level:
   a. voice inflection and hand gestures
   b. smiles
   c. body language and touch
   *d. all of the above
   Page: 74

8. Which of the following tends to be the most important nonverbal form?
   a. eye contact
   *b. appearance
   c. voice
   d. All of the above are equally weighted.
   Page: 74

9. The significance of appearance to communication rests in the fact that
   a. first impressions are largely based on appearance.
   b. self-perceptions regarding appearance affect one's self-confidence.
   *c. both a and b
   d. neither a nor b
   Page: 74

10. People perceived as physically attractive typically are also perceived as all of the following EXCEPT
    a. smart.
    *b. independent.
    c. sociable.
    d. successful.
    Page: 75

11. Competent communicators should practice which of the following?
    a. considering the impact of their appearance on how they are perceived
    b. trying to rely less on physical appearance in forming impressions of another person
    c. considering the degree to which their appearance is appropriate to the context of communication
    *d. all of the above
    Page: 76

12. Research indicates that the face signals which of the following emotions with a high degree of meaning?
    *a. happiness, surprise, fear, anger, disgust, contempt, sadness, interest
    b. surprise, fear, boredom, anger
    c. appreciation, surprise, fear, anger, disappointment
    d. happiness, surprise, sadness, shyness
    Page: 76

13. Oculesics is the study of
    a. body language.
    *b. eye behavior.
    c. vocalic behavior.
    d. touch.
    Page: 77

14. Research indicates that most people believe they can deduce which of the following based on someone's voiceprint?
    a. age
    b. race
    c. character-defining traits
    *d. all of the above
    Page: 77

15. Kinesics is the study of
    a. how people use and respond to touch.
    *b. movement.
    c. eye behavior.
    d. space, distance, and territory.
    Page: 78

16. Self-adapters are common gestures that
    a. help communicators add to what the face tells us about an emotion they are experiencing.
    *b. help people compensate for feelings of anxiety.
    c. help individuals to control interactions more effectively.
    d. all of the above
    Page: 79

17. Some environments are _____ , meaning they stimulate human involvement, whereas others may be _____ , meaning they are configured to make people feel distant.
    a. sociofugal; sociopetal
    *b. sociopetal; sociofugal
    Page: 82

18. Personal-distance norms are a consequence of all of the following EXCEPT
    a. culture.
    *b. past experiences.
    c. relationships.
    d. all of the above
    Page: 82

19. People who feel their personal-distance norms have been violated typically respond in which way?
    a. use the flight response
    b. stand their ground
    c. objectify the violator
    *d. all of the above
    Page: 83

20. The study of time is technically called
    a. proxemics.
    b. oculesics.
    *c. chronemics.
    d. kinesics.
    Page: 83

21. Nonverbal behaviors frequently mistaken for flirting, such as eye contact, primping, touching, and blushing, are referred to as
    a. decoys.
    *b. quasi-courtship behaviors.
    c. pseudo-attraction indicators.
    d. haptics.
    Page: 88

22. Cross-modality checking refers to
    a. comparing findings from oculesics, kinesics, haptics, proxemics, and chronemics endeavors.
    *b. comparing channels of communication in the attempt to determine a message's meaning.
    c. using feedback to check the accuracy of interpretations between the sender and the receiver of communication.
    d. communicating through more than one nonverbal behavior simultaneously.
    Page: 89

23. To successfully self-monitor your nonverbal communication, you need to follow which set of steps?
    *a. (1) recognize important cues; (2) interpret those cues once you recognize them; (3) analyze the potential consequences of your response; and (4) respond appropriately to those cues
    b. (1) commit to engaging in self-monitoring behavior in all communication transactions; (2) observe receivers' response to your nonverbal messages; (3) determine if altering your nonverbal messages is warranted; (4) analyze the potential consequences of adapting your nonverbal message or failing to do so; (5) decide on a course of action
    c. (1) recognize receivers' nonverbal cues; (2) seek clarification of your interpretation of those cues; (3) determine your response and its potential consequences; (4) choose to adapt or not adapt nonverbal messages
    d. none of the above
    Page: 91

True/False

24. Research indicates that the face is rich in nonverbal cues which signal the intensity of emotions and the degree of control people have over their emotions. (True, p. 77)

25. Researchers believe that, compared to the face, the voice is easy to manipulate in an attempt to project a certain image. (True, p. 78)

26. Haptics helps us to understand people's use of common gestures. (False, p. 79)

27. A person's gestures and movements usually are spontaneous yet formal, reflecting the content of a message, but not necessarily the context of communication. (False, p. 79)

28. Haptics is the most intimate of the codes in the nonverbal system. (True, p. 79)

29. Research supports that women are much better at interpreting nonverbal communication than men. (True, p. 87)

30. Research supports that 90 percent of the meaning of a message is attributable to nonverbal behavior. (False, p. 88)

31. When verbal and nonverbal messages appear to contradict one another, we generally believe the latter. (True, p. 89)

32. Immediacy involves people's perception of how close they are to others. (True, p. 93)

Short Answer/Essay

33. The authors of your text explain that people have criteria they use to judge other people's physical attractiveness. How does this affect how they see themselves and their overall communication competence? (p. 75)

34. Explain the statement "Low-status people tolerate much nonreciprocal behavior from high-status people in the workplace." Cite specific examples. (p. 80)

35. Define and explain the terms *sociopetal* and *sociofugal*. (p. 82)

36. Professor Dale Leathers believes nonverbal messages communicated through our appearance, face and eyes, voice, touch, space, and time interact to perform what six major functions? (p. 85)

37. Explain the term *metacommunication*. (p. 86)

38. Explain three common misconceptions about nonverbal communication. (p. 87)

CHAPTER 5
ETHICAL COMMUNICATION

INTRODUCTION AND OUTLINE

Chapter 5 begins what will become the ongoing discussion of ethics and their close relationship to communication. In this chapter, students learn a variety of perspectives that help them to understand why ethical behavior seems to vary across cultures and sometimes even classrooms. Furthermore, students receive numerous ethical norms and guidelines they should employ in their quest to become more competent communicators. Specifically, Chapter 5 discusses:

I. Perspectives that help us to understand ethics
   A. **Ethical relativism** describes the notion that a person's career, profession, culture, or belief system excuses him or her from complying with any universal code of conduct.
   B. **Universal rules** are universal ethical standards that transcend any group or culture.
      1. Immanual Kant proposed the categorical imperative: "Act only on that maxim through which you can at the same time will that it should become a universal law." This perspective is a way to deduce fundamental ethical rules from one basic principle that he believes is self-evident regardless of one's individual or cultural background.
      2. Kant also proposed, "Act in such a way that you always treat humanity whether in your own person or in the person of any other, never simply as a means, but always at the same time as an end." This simply means to treat people with respect, not simply as a means of achieving our goals.
   C. **Utilitarianism** seeks the greatest good (happiness) for the greatest number.
   D. **Situational ethics** describes the belief that there are overriding ethical maxims, but that sometimes it is necessary to set them aside to fulfill a higher law.
   E. **Ethical means vs. ethical ends** is a struggle for many, but competent communicators recognize that ethical communication requires both. Competent communicators base their behavior on its probable consequences not only for themselves, but also for others who will be affected. They do not believe that ethical ends justify unethical means.

II. Ethical norms for communication are based on the following:
   A. **Universality of truthfulness** is a universal norm to which competent communicators subscribe with rare exceptions.
   B. **Respect for the power of language** and its potentially destructive use guides competent communicators to choose their words wisely.
   C. **Tolerance for differences** guides the competent communicator to recognize that the customary criteria they use in judging what is ethical may be inappropriate in judging the degree to which other people's behavior is ethical.
   D. **Good reasons** must be offered for believing, valuing, and acting. Good reasons are messages, based on moral principles, offered in support of propositions concerning what we should believe or how we should act.

E. **Interaction consciousness** requires competent communicators to try to balance the satisfaction of their needs with those of the people with whom they come into contact.

III. Ethical guidelines for sources and receivers
   A. Following are ethical guidelines for sources.
      1. **Attribution** concerns giving credit to people whose ideas you either directly quote or borrow from liberally.
      2. **Giving good reasons** means gaining compliance from people through appealing to the best, not the worst, in people.
      3. **Creating conditions for informed choice** requires the source to provide others with all of the information necessary for them to make sound and principled decisions.
      4. **Balancing freedom of speech and the power of words** leads competent communicators to weigh their words prior to speaking because they understand that the best way to protect freedom of speech is through ethical communication behavior.
   B. Ethical guidelines for receivers include:
      1. **Accepting responsibility for the choices they make** during and following a communication transaction.
      2. **Keeping themselves informed** on issues of the day because ignorance is no excuse for unethical behavior.
      3. **Speaking up** when convinced that a source of communication is misinforming or misleading people.
      4. **Admitting that as receivers we have a subjective view** that may bias how we receive and process a source's message.
   C. The ethical norms of truthfulness, respect for the power of language, tolerance, good reasons, and interaction consciousness oblige communicators to behave ethically regardless of whether they are the source or the receiver.

IV. The dialogic imperative
   A. This dimension of rhetorical sensitivity involves the communicator's commitment to consider his or her needs relative to those of others.
   B. Two scholars cited in the text expanded on the idea of dialogic ethics.
      1. Martin Buber believes we are nothing by ourselves but are the products of our relationships with others and the messages we share. As a result, he believes that we are ethically obligated to communicate in such a way that it nurtures the relationship between us and other people.
      2. Richard Johannesen developed some specific guidelines designed to assist communicators in nurturing their relationships with others, and therefore, themselves.
         a. **Authenticity** requires the communicators to present genuine representations of themselves to others, rather than trying to manipulate their behavior to achieve some calculated impression.
         b. **Inclusion** involves communication behaviors that assist people feeling significant and worthwhile.
         c. **Confirmation** involves communication behaviors that tell people that what they think and what they say counts, even when others disagree.
         d. **Presentness** means we are listening intently to the other person.

e. **Mutual equality** means that those involved in the relationship are partners with equal say and influence.

f. **Supportiveness** requires creating a relational climate based on cooperation and mutual respect.

TEACHING/LEARNING OBJECTIVES

After reading Chapter 5, your students should be able to:

- Explain why ethical behavior is important for everyone in every context of communication.

- Identify some of the key ethical questions facing today's communicators.

- Understand the importance of committing to personally engaging in ethical communication.

- Recognize the norms to which competent communicators subscribe.

- Identify the differences between ethical and unethical communication.

- Recognize there are times when there are exceptions to the "rules."

- Practice the obligations and responsibilities of ethical communicators.

- Discuss the ways that being an ethical communicator overlaps with being rhetorically and culturally sensitive.

- Comprehend the seriousness of engaging in plagiarism and other unethical acts.

- Meet the learning objectives listed on page 97 in the text.

TROUBLESHOOTING

The discussion of ethical communication invites interesting conversation and opposing viewpoints. Many instructors find the study of ethics and its close relationship to communication difficult to teach. The difficulty lies in the absence of absolute truth—an issue that ultimately arises in the debate between what is right and wrong.

Be prepared to answer student questions such as:

- Who has the right to decide what is right or wrong for someone else to say or do?

- When some perceive an abuse of the right to freedom of expression, is the answer unlimited freedoms, censorship, or something in between? Who decides? Who is best equipped to decide?

- Who decides which groups are the hatemongers or those others that should be quieted or silenced? (Consider that both the United States and France won their independence from monarchies. What if the revolutionaries had been silenced as the monarchy wanted?)

- Whose universal code of conduct are we supposed to follow?

- Can we get along in a global community when differing philosophies abound?

When teaching ethical communication, instructors need to keep in mind the possible differing views held by students in a multicultural classroom. Furthermore, they should avoid dogmatically espousing their own views.

INSTRUCTIONAL EXERCISES

1. Engage students in a brainstorming activity to compile a list of ethical behaviors they believe to be universals in terms of ethical communication. This list could become a code of conduct for your classroom which they created and thus feel responsible for. Instructors could then lead the students to further discuss exceptions to these "universals." This exercise could reinforce the idea that competent communicators abide by norms and recognize universals, but that they also believe there may be exceptions that will more fully benefit all of those involved in the communication transaction.

2. Throughout Chapter 5, Scott and Brydon provide many examples in which those involved failed to act in an ethical manner. Have student groups engage in a brainstorming activity to come up with current relevant examples of people demonstrating ethical behavior or lack thereof. This exercise can be extended to include an opportunity for members to become a task-oriented group and create a possible solution for dealing with such unethical behavior.

   In teams of three, have students work in the library to find documentation of recent ethical or unethical publicized events. Ask teams to present a balanced three-minute informative speech on the event.

   Have students search the Internet and find an address where they believe the information presented abuses our right to freedom of expression. In groups of three or four, have students share their findings and their reasoning for selecting this information for this particular assignment. Following, ask students to discuss if there is an appropriate place to share this information.

JOURNAL WRITING

Identify someone that you consider to be an ethical person. In a journal entry, consider the characteristics or behaviors that lead to this belief. Further explore what you wish to emulate in order to meet one class objective of becoming a more ethical communicator. Next, repeat this exercise exploring unethical characteristics and behaviors.

DISCUSSION TOPICS

On page 101, Scott and Brydon state that history is replete with cases demonstrating that it's sometimes better to bend the truth. The authors cite those brave individuals who helped to hide the Jewish people during Nazi Germany as an example. Initiate a class discussion regarding the topic of when it is right to lie. Further probe about how one can be sure that he or she is doing the right thing.

Scott and Brydon explain that competent communicators understand that the best way to protect freedom of speech is through ethical communication behavior. When the standards for ethical communication are not upheld, would you promote censorship? To any degree? Under any circumstances?

When discussing ethical relativism, initiate a conversation that revolves around a cultural practice which North Americans may tend to find unethical (e.g., bullfights in Spain, genital mutilation and the killing of baby girls in some countries). What can we as a society do about the cultural practice? How about as an individual? Should we try to impose our views on their culture? Could we be successful? If so, how?

Two weeks before the TWA flight 800 disaster in July of 1996, a FBI report indicated that explosive-like substances were not detected on FBI agents posing as passengers. Should the U.S. government have made this information available to the American public? Were they acting unethically in not doing so?

How do you feel about burning the flag as exercising one's right to freedom of expression?

How do you feel about the availability of pornography on the Internet? Home pages for hate groups? The fact that some on-line chat services have a company employee or "guide" that ends certain discussions and language in chat rooms?

TEST QUESTIONS

Multiple Choice

1. The notion that one's career or profession, culture or belief system excuses him or her from complying with any universal code of conduct is known as
   a. ethnocentrism.
   *b. ethical relativism.
   c. utilitarianism.
   d. situational ethics.
   Page: 100

2. "Act in such a way that you always treat humanity whether in your own person or in the person of any other, never simply as a means, but always at the same time as an end" was said by
   a. Aristotle.
   b. Scott and Brydon.
   *c. Kant.
   d. Johannesen.
   Page: 100

3. The position that there are no universal ethical principles is called
   a. situational ethics.
   *b. ethical relativism.
   c. cultural relativism.
   d. ethical tolerance.
   Page: 100

4. The ethical principle of the greatest amount of happiness for the greatest number of people is known as
   a. ethnocentrism.
   b. interaction consciousness.
   *c. utilitarianism.
   d. dialogic ethics.
   Page: 101

5. Situational ethics can best be described as
   a. inevitably discriminating against some minority group when seeking the greatest good for the greatest number.
   *b. believing that there are overriding ethical maxims, but that sometimes it is necessary to set them aside in particular situations to fulfill a higher law.
   c. basing one's behavior on its probable consequences for oneself or those others affected.
   d. believing that your ethical standards may be different than the ethical standards of people from other cultures.
   Page: 102

6. The authors of your text suggest that ethical norms be based on
   a. ethical relativism; universal rules; utilitarianism; and situational ethics.
   *b. universality of truthfulness; respect for the power of language; tolerance for differences; reasons and the situation; and interaction consciousness.
   c. weighing ethical means vs. ethical ends.
   d. the greatest good for the greatest number.
   Page: 103

7. Ethical norms for communication competence are based on all of the following EXCEPT
   a. the universality of truthfulness.
   b. interaction consciousness.
   *c. utilitarianism.
   d. tolerances for differences.
   Page: 103

8. The universal norm of truthfulness which competent communicators subscribe to dictates that
   a. sometimes the truth is best withheld.
   b. truthfulness is important to communication competence regardless of the context.
   *c. both a and b
   d. neither a nor b
   Page: 104

9. Language is characterized as all of the following EXCEPT
   a. powerful in its own right.
   *b. neutral.
   c. potentially constructive depending on the communicator.
   d. potentially destructive depending on the communicator.
   Page: 104

10. Statements based on moral principles, and offered in support of propositions concerning what we should believe or how we should act, are known as:
    *a. good reasons.
    b. categorical imperatives.
    c. haptics.
    d. attributes.
    Page: 106

11. _____ believed that communicators must offer each other "good reasons" for believing, valuing, and acting.
    a. Immanual Kant
    *b. Karl Wallace
    c. Plato
    d. Bill Moyers
    Page: 106

12. Interaction consciousness can best be described as
    a. Karl Wallace's notion of being rhetorically sensitive.
    *b. balancing the satisfaction of one's own needs with the needs of others one interacts with.
    c. becoming aware that communicators have the responsibility to provide one another support to believe, value, or act.
    d. all of the above
    Page: 107

13. Attribution can be described as all of the following EXCEPT
    a. a responsibility of the source of communication.
    b. giving credit to people that you borrow from.
    *c. your responsibility in writing but not necessarily in public speaking.
    d. a responsibility of the receiver.
    Page: 107

    (Students may often choose D. However, Scott and Brydon state on page 111 that it is the receiver's ethical responsibility to speak up when convinced that a source of communication is misinforming or misleading the people and specifically state this may be the case when one passes off another's ideas as their own.)

14. When politicians omit relevant information regarding a debated issue with which they aim to gain public agreement, the _____ responsibility of _____ has been violated.
    a. sender's; providing good reasons
    b. receiver's; keeping themselves informed
    *c. sender's; creating conditions of informed choice
    d. source's; attribution
    Page: 108

15. All of the following are specific guidelines for engaging in Johannesen dialogic ethics EXCEPT
    a. presentness.
    b. authenticity.
    c. mutual equality.
    *d. sincerity.
    Page: 112

True/False

16. In short, ethics is the study of right and wrong and its relationship to communication. (True, p. 97)

17. The notion that one's career, culture, or belief system excuses him or her from complying with any universal code of conduct is exemplary of ethical relativism. (True, p. 100)

18. According to the authors of your text, North Americans historically have been more tolerant of conflicting beliefs and behaviors than many other cultures primarily because North America was built on the melting pot theory. (False, p. 106).

19. Credibility is established based primarily on one's trustworthiness (False, p. 104)

20. Language can be considered neutral, but people's uses of it can be beneficial or destructive. (False, p. 104)

21. Competent communicators often agree that ethical ends justify ethical means. (False, p. 106)

22. Immigrants who accede to North American norms are quickly assimilated. (True, p. 106)

23. In regard to ethics, tolerance for differences suggests that one must approve of ethical norms other than one's own. (False, p. 106)

24. Interaction consciousness means thinking about the relational consequences of communication behavior. (True, p. 107)

25. In small group situations, interaction consciousness can be interpreted to mean that the needs of individuals often need to prevail over group pressures. (False, p. 107)

26. People who find themselves in the primary role of sender have a greater ethical responsibility than those who occupy the primary role of receiver. (False, p. 108)

27. In many cases, ignorance serves as an acceptable excuse for unethical behavior. (False, p. 111)

28. Perception is colored by one's experience both real and vicarious. (True, p. 111)

Short Answer/Essay

29. The authors of your text explain that ethics is the study of right and wrong and its relationship to communication. Explain the idea/statement and its relationship to communication. (p. 107)

30. Explain why critics of utilitarianism say that it promotes ethical relativism. (p. 100)

31. The authors suggest that one must always be mindful about the degree to which the ethical standards from communication in your own culture generalize to a culture with which you have little or no familiarity. When suggesting to be mindful, are the authors suggesting that "when in Rome do as the Romans"? If not, then what should one do when one's ethical standards for communication conflict with those of another culture? (p. 106)

32. Explain why the authors are "committed to the belief that ethical behavior is the cornerstone of communication competence." (p. 98)

33. Explain the speaker's responsibility of "creating conditions for informed choice." (p. 108)

34. The authors list several examples to demonstrate the idea of interaction consciousness. Explain the term *interaction consciousness* and provide an example of how this idea can be interpreted in some specific communication context. (pp. 106–107)

35. List and explain the source's and the receiver's ethical responsibilities. (pp. 107–111)

CHAPTER 6
LISTENING AND CRITICAL THINKING

INTRODUCTION AND OUTLINE

Listening and critical thinking are coupled in Chapter 6 because of their dependent nature. To be an effective critical thinker, one must be an effective listener. To be an effective listener, one must employ critical thinking skills. Chapter 6 provides numerous opportunities to demonstrate to students how communication concepts and skills, specifically regarding effective listening and critical thinking, frequent our day-to-day experiences. Scott and Brydon discuss:

I. The nature of listening
   A. Hearing is not the same as listening.
      1. Hearing is a physical process.
      2. Listening is both physical and mental and can be active or passive.
   B. Listening requires consciously receiving, attending to, and assigning meaning to verbal and nonverbal messages.
   C. Most scholars also agree that listening involves:
      1. selective attention—attending to messages we perceive to be reinforcing;
      2. sensorial involvement—listening with all applicable senses, not simply the sense of hearing;
      3. comprehension; and
      4. retention.

II. Three common myths about listening
   A. It's easy to listen.
   B. Smart people are better listeners.
   C. There's no need to plan ahead.

III. Six important obstacles to listening
   A. Carrying on an **internal dialogue** in response to another's words affects our ability to listen.
   B. The **physical environment** such as noise, temperature, and lighting affects our ability to listen.
   C. **Cultural differences** in communication patterns such as eye contact and verbal encouragers or lack thereof affect our ability to listen.
   D. **Personal problems** may preoccupy and prevent someone from listening effectively.
   E. **Bias** is a serious impediment to listening.
   F. Understanding that people may have very different **connotations** for the same word is essential to promoting effective listening.

IV. Types of listening
   A. **Discriminative listening** involves learning to distinguish among the variety of verbal and nonverbal cues to which we are exposed.
   B. **Comprehensive listening** is listening targeted at understanding. How well you comprehensively listen depends on several factors:

1. vocabulary
2. concentration
   a. wide-band
   b. pinpoint
3. memory

C. **Appreciative listening** is listening for enjoyment.

D. **Therapeutic listening** means helping people in a nonevaluative and non-threatening way to express their feelings.

E. **Critical listening** is listening to make reasoned judgment about the communicator and message.
   1. Learning to listen critically is a form of self-protection. By listening critically, we can learn the critical questions to ask so that we can guard ourselves against being taken advantage of by unscrupulous people.
   2. Learning to listen critically will also enhance our ability to communicate with others because it will force us to apply a similar set of critical questions to ourselves before speaking.

V. Listening skills

A. You must consciously choose to practice effective listening.

B. Nine techniques of effective listening are:
   1. setting goals
   2. blocking out distracting stimuli
   3. suspending judgment
   4. focusing on main points
   5. recognizing highlights and signposts
   6. taking effective notes
   7. being sensitive to the meta-message, or the message about the message
   8. paraphrasing
   9. questioning

VI. Critical listening and thinking

A. **Critical thinking** involves making sound inferences based on accurate evidence and valid reasoning.

B. Toulmin developed a model of argument that is helpful in understanding the relationship between critical listening and critical thinking.
   1. The model has the following three main parts:
      a. claim—a conclusion the arguer wishes to establish
      b. grounds—evidence to support the claim
      c. warrant—a linkage between the grounds and claim
   2. The following three additional features may be present in the argument:
      a. backing—further support to the warrant
      b. rebuttal—a counterargument
      c. qualifier—says the claim must be considered in light of certain exceptions
   3. The critical thinker must guard against fallacies.

A. A fallacy is an argument that appears sound at first glance but contains a flaw in reasoning that makes it unsound.

B. The following are eight common fallacies to watch out for:
   1. unsupported assertion
   2. distorted evidence

3. faulty opinion evidence
4. hasty generalization
5. false analogy
6. post hoc reasoning and mistaking correlation for cause
7. slippery slope
8. non sequitur

TEACHING/LEARNING OBJECTIVES

After reading Chapter 6, your students should:

- Be convinced of the importance of effective listening and critical thinking in all communication transactions.

- Understand that effective listening is not easy but a skill that can be improved with practice.

- Be assured that potential employers value effective listening and critical thinking skills.

- Recognize helpful and harmful listening and thinking behaviors.

- Cite specific examples of instances where they were effective or ineffective in using their listening or critical thinking skills.

- Identify and apply strategies that help improve one's competence in effective listening and critical thinking.

- Set goals for improving their listening skills.

- Determine a method for personally evaluating listening behavior.

- Meet the learning objectives listed on page 117 in the text.

TROUBLESHOOTING

Students' Attitudes

Chapter 6 covers effective listening and critical thinking areas that are taken less than seriously by many students. You may hear comments such as, "I listen every day, therefore I'm already good at it" or "I don't need you to teach me how to think."

Part of your challenge in Chapter 6 is to clearly demonstrate (1) how prevalent ineffective listening is in all of our daily lives; (2) how valued effective listening and critical thinking skills are in this society; (3) that the objective is not to change how students think but to eliminate practices and thought processes that they already know (on some level) are ineffective; and (4) how easy it is to be misled when not engaging in critical thinking.

Testing

A second challenge facing you is that testing recall of facts and concepts about effective listening is easy, but testing application of skills is difficult. As a result, this can become a less focused upon subject area despite it being one of the most important lessons we can teach. The challenge is to create an environment where effective listening skills are practiced and evaluated inside and outside the classroom every day, not only on the day(s) when discussion revolves around effective listening. Some suggestions include:

- Make it a practice, beginning on the first day of class, to frequently ask students to restate or summarize discussion material or classmates/instructor's comments.

- Ask students to develop an impromptu speech that involves an instance in which their listening was either effective or ineffective.

- Add an element to student speech critique sheets which requires reviewers to briefly summarize main ideas or supporting information presented.

- Require students to listen to and review major speeches (political debates, the State of the Union address or the State of the State address) and to present a brief summary to the class in a creative manner.

Vocabulary

Passive listening may be confusing for some of your students. It is described in the text as not mindless but not as mindful as active listening. Point out to your students that passive learning means that the receiver hopes the sender is exceptionally clear and honest because little or no effort is exerted by the receiver. It means the receiver is counting on not needing critical listening or thinking skills.

INSTRUCTIONAL EXERCISES

1. One teaching objective aims to help students understand that effective listening requires learning a skill. Examples of ineffective listening surface in our everyday encounters. To demonstrate this point, remind students of the game "Telephone" which most everyone played in elementary school. Then tell them that today they will play a variation of the original game. They will have a lot of fun with this.

   To complete the exercise:

   - Create a short story (about a minute long) that includes events, people, and some specific details.

   - Solicit five volunteers.

   - Take the volunteers out in the hallway to explain the procedure and rules of the game (this heightens the attention level of the audience).

     - The rules are simple: they need to listen and are not allowed to ask questions.

     - The procedure is as follows:

       (1) Read a short story to the first volunteer in front of the entire audience while the remaining volunteers wait outside and out of hearing distance.

       (2) After you have read the story to the first volunteer, bring in the second volunteer who will receive the story from the first volunteer in front of the entire audience.

       (3) Have the second volunteer tell the story to the third volunteer and so on until ultimately the fifth volunteer tells the story to the audience

Discussion regarding this exercise should include but is not limited to:

- Lost details of the story.
  This becomes an excellent opportunity to point out that these students knew that their listening skills were going to be tested and yet the story got distorted.

- Parts of the story that did not get lost.
  Discuss the fact that individuals typically remember things that are important to them personally (e.g., details about money, job position, the gender of the people involved and possibly names).

- Changed details.
  This demonstrates that we tend to "fill in the blanks" when a story seems incomplete or details seem incongruent.

- The fact that we all listen, sometimes believe, and maybe even repeat accounts that were told from a friend by another friend and so on.

2. Scott and Brydon indicate that there are a number of common myths about effective listening and list the following three: (1) it's easy to listen; (2) smart people are better listeners; and (3) there's no need to plan ahead. Engage the class in a brainstorming activity to introduce the topic or to extend the list of misconceptions. You may want to list the class's contributions on the blackboard. Possible myths to add to this list include:

- Listening is the same activity as hearing.

- Understanding comes simply from paying attention.

Consider as a variation breaking students into small groups to engage in this brainstorming activity before engaging in class discussion.

3. Scott and Brydon indicate that there are a number of barriers to effective listening and list the following six as the most important, meaning the most common, obstacles: (1) the internal dialogue to which we are prone; (2) physical conditions; (3) cultural differences; (4) personal problems; (5) prejudices; and (6) connotative meanings. Engage the class in a brainstorming activity to extend the list of barriers to effective listening.

The list of additional obstacles to effective listening could include

- holding predispositions or creating self-fulfilling prophecies (e.g., "I heard this class was really boring");

- lacking interest in the subject of the message;

- losing focus;

- rehearsing a response when you should be listening;

- engaging in bad habits (e.g., learning how to look attentive when you are really thinking about something else);

- being lazy because the material is complex or lengthy;

- prejudging the communication or the communicator.

Consider as a variation breaking students into small groups to engage in this brainstorming activity before engaging in class discussion.

4. In small groups, have students compile a list of words that they define differently than their parents, grandparents, or teachers do. After students define each term from each standpoint, provide them with a dictionary to compare their variations of connotative meanings to the denotative meanings.

JOURNAL WRITING

Consider an instance in which you failed to employ your critical thinking skills. What was the situation and the end result? How did you feel at that time? Based on what you have learned in Chapter 6, is there anything that you would do differently? What can you do to avoid a similar situation in the future?

DISCUSSION TOPICS

Discuss the general importance of effective listening. Ask class members to recall incidents when they were not listened to and how it made them feel. Also discuss a case where they made a mistake because they didn't truly listen to someone else. Point out how much more time is spent listening than in any other communication activity.

Discuss the importance of listening in a class that focuses on public speaking. This is a good time to explicitly discuss norms of audience behavior. How will students feel as speakers if their audience is inattentive? Also, how can a speaker, through use of repetition, redundancy, and so forth, overcome the known obstacles to effective listening?

Discuss effective note-taking. You might ask students to take notes on one of your lectures and turn them in to you. Then discuss your lecture in terms of the main point you were trying to convey versus what appeared in the students' notes on that lecture.

Discuss the importance of critical thinking in the communication transaction from the points of view of both the sender and the consumer of information. It is often useful to bring in examples of advertisements that appear to be strong on reasoning. Discuss the types of reasoning employed in the advertisements and how strong the reasoning appears to be. Point out the fallacies, if any, that are included.

TEST QUESTIONS

Multiple Choice

1. People spend approximately _____ of their communication time listening and _____ speaking.
   a. 14%; 65%
   *b. 53%; 16%
   c. 25%; 25%
   d. 65%; 14%
   Page: 118

2. Listening can be described as which of the following?
   a. physical and mental
   b. active
   c. passive
   *d. all of the above
   Page: 119

3. Sensorial involvement describes
   a. engaging in the process of active listening instead of passive listening.
   *b. listening with all applicable senses.
   c. carrying on an internal dialogue in response to another's words.
   d. overcoming all physical obstacles in the environment that might affect one's ability to listen.
   Page: 119

4. Immediately after something has been said, the average listener remembers about
   a. 85%.
   b. 70%.
   *c. 50%.
   d. 30%.
   Page: 119

5. After 48 hours of something being said, the average listener remembers approximately
   a. 60%.
   b. 45%.
   *c. 25%.
   d. 15%.
   Page: 119

6. Jim and Rob are really trying to do well in their speech communication course. During lecture, they engage in activities such as sitting in the front row, leaning forward in their desks, taking notes, and watching the instructor's nonverbal signals. These activities are best described by the idea of
   a. selective attention.
   *b. sensorial involvement.
   c. comprehending meaning.
   d. retaining and remembering.
   Page: 119

7. Every message has the following dimensions:
   *a. content and relationship
   b. task and social
   c. relationship and task
   d. content and delivery
   Page: 120

8. The fact that we are more likely to give our individual attention to someone whose message reflects our views rather than opposes them is best explained by
   a. self-fulfilling prophecy.
   b. sensorial involvement.

c. discriminative listening.

*d. selective attention.

Page: 120

9. Listening improves with all of the following EXCEPT

    a. increased selective attention.

    *b. intelligence.

    c. sensorial involvement.

    d. planning.

    Page: 121

10. All of the following are common myths about effective listening EXCEPT

    a. listening automatically results from intelligence.

    *b. listening is different from hearing.

    c. listening does not require planning.

    d. listening is easy.

    Page: 121

11. Which of the following can hinder one's ability to effectively listen?

    a. poor lighting

    b. personal problems

    *c. both a and b

    d. neither a nor b

    Page: 122

12. Which of the following is NOT an obstacle to listening?

    a. internal dialogues

    *b. planning for listening

    c. physical conditions

    d. cultural differences

    Page: 122

13. The authors of your text list one's internal dialogue as an obstacle to effective listening. All of the following are true about this dialogue EXCEPT that

    a. it is prevalent under conditions of stress.

    *b. it is always an obstacle to effective listening.

    c. it includes behavior like rehearsing your response when you should be listening.

    d. it is one reason we fail to remember people's names.

    Page: 122

14. According to the text, which of the following are the most common and therefore the most important obstacles to listening which we must strive to overcome?

    a. external noise; internal noise; lack of intelligence to comprehend; ethnocentric attitudes

    *b. internal dialogue; physical conditions; cultural differences; personal problems; prejudices; connotative meanings

    c. internal noise; selective attention; the communication environment; differences with the communication sender

    d. none of the above

    Page: 122

15. Connotative meanings can best be described as
    a. literal interpretations.
    *b. sometimes unshared interpretations that people have for verbal and nonverbal signs and symbols.
    c. meanings given to words in the dictionary.
    d. meanings requiring translation from another language.
    Page: 126

16. Comprehensive listening is
    a. listening targeted at distinguishing verbal and nonverbal cues from one another.
    *b. listening targeted at understanding.
    c. listening with all applicable senses.
    d. engaging in active versus passive listening.
    Page: 127

17. In an attempt to suspend judgment, the authors of your text suggest all of the following EXCEPT
    a. recognizing that everyone brings subjective experiences to the communication transaction.
    b. avoiding "judging a book by its cover."
    c. separating the message from the communicator.
    *d. focusing on highlights and signposts.
    Page: 136

18. Which of the following strategies do the authors of your text suggest for effective note-taking?
    *a. being sensitive to meta-communication
    b. blocking out distracting stimuli
    c. suspending judgment
    d. all of the above
    Page: 137

19. Being sensitive to meta-communication, paraphrasing, and questioning are all strategies the authors of your text suggest for
    a. avoiding hasty judgments.
    *b. effective note taking.
    c. improving listening skills.
    d. recognizing fallacies.
    Page: 137

20. What part of the Toulmin model acts as linkage, connecting the grounds with the claim?
    a. qualifier
    b. backing
    c. rebuttal
    *d. warrant
    Page: 140

21. Which of the following parts of the Toulmin model of argument represents the point the arguer is tying to prove?
*a. claim
b. warrant
c. grounds
d. backing
Page: 141

22. Which of the following parts of the Toulmin model represents the degree of certainty the arguer has in an argument?
a. rebuttal
b. grounds
*c. modal qualifier
d. none of the above
Page: 141

23. When significant omissions or changes in the ground of an argument are used to alter the argument's original intent, which fallacy has been committed?
a. unsupported assertion
*b. distorted evidence
c. false analogy
d. post hoc
Page: 141

24. Which of the following is NOT a common type of fallacy?
a. distorted evidence.
*b. analogy.
c. post hoc reasoning.
d. unsupported assertion.
Page: 141

25. A non sequitur is
a. the assumption that a series of undesirable events will result from a single action.
b. reasoning which overgeneralizes based on insufficient evidence.
*c. a claim that does not follow from its premise.
d. none of the above
Page: 145

True/False

26. After about 48 hours, the average listener remembers only half of a message. (False, p. 119)

27. The activity of listening begins when the sender of the message engages in audience analysis to craft a message that is easy for the receiver to process. (False, p. 119)

28. Professional listeners, such as therapists, typically engage in passive listening since they tend to listen closely without responding frequently. (False, p. 119)

29. Since we listen to others every day, we do not need to practice our listening skills. (False, p. 120)

30. Meta-messages are generally conveyed nonverbally. (True, pp. 137–138)

31. Hearing and listening are basically the same activity. (False, pp. 127–129)

32. Studies indicate that most people are inclined to attend to messages that they find contradictory to their own beliefs or perceptions in order to better understand the situation for discussion purposes. (False, p. 127)

33. One's ability to listen directly affects one's intelligence. (False, pp. 121–122)

34. Comprehensive listening involves sorting out the array of verbal and nonverbal messages that are simultaneously delivered to transmit a complete message. (False, pp. 127–129)

35. Appreciative listening involves empathetic listening. (False, p. 130)

36. The absence of grounds to support a claim is best known as the non sequitur fallacy. (False, p. 145)

Short Answer/Essay

37. Construct an argument and label its parts using the Toulmin model. (pp. 140–142)

38. List and explain the six common obstacles to listening as discussed in Chapter 6. (pp. 122–126)

39. Contrast selective attention and sensorial involvement. Provide specific examples of each. (pp. 119–120)

40. Create an argument which commits the slippery slope fallacy. (p. 144)

41. Compare and contrast listening and critical listening. (pp. 132–134)

CHAPTER 7
COMMUNICATION AND DIVERSITY

INTRODUCTION AND OUTLINE

Diversity is all around us, and it is continuing to grow. Chapter 7 focuses on teaching students how to become more competent communicators by incorporating diversity-responsive communication into their everyday lives. Specifically, the chapter covers:

I. Perception and Attribution
   A. Perception is the process by which we give meaning to experience.
      1. It is easily biased by experience or the lack thereof.
      2. Inexperience with cultures, groups, or individual backgrounds dissimilar to our own can lead to perceptual bias and inaccurate attributions about the diverse people we come in contact with.
   B. Attributions are the reasons we give to explain our own behaviors and the behaviors of others.
      1. The more similar people are to us, the more accurate the attributions we make about them.
      2. The more dissimilar people are to us, the less accurate the attributions we make about them.
   C. Perceptual bias and inaccurate attributions are likely when we come in contact with someone from a different cultural background because of **ethnocentrism.** When ethnocentric, we are predisposed to perceive our own culture as superior to others.

II. Three Levels of Diversity: Cultural, Group, and Individual
   A. Culture is the collective pattern of thinking, feeling, and acting characteristic of a specific human society. It includes history, literature, music, greeting, eating, showing or not showing feelings, keeping a certain physical distance from others, making love, and maintaining body hygiene.
      1. **Cultural literacy** is the ability to interpret and appropriately respond to the communication behaviors of people from other cultures.
      2. Communication scholar Geert Hofstede says that all cultures are characterized by four value dimensions:
         a. collectivism and individualism
            (1) All cultures fall somewhere on the continuum between collectivism and individualism.
            (2) Collectivistic cultures believe the good of the many far outweighs the good of the few.
            (3) In highly individualistic countries, communication is frequently competitive.
         b. power distance
            (1) This dimension concerns the degree to which inequality exists and how it affects people.

      (2) When communicating with people from cultures other than your own, it's a good idea to learn about and respect both the sources of power within a culture and the manner in which power is typically acquired.

    c. uncertainty avoidance

      (1) Just as people vary in terms of the amount of uncertainty they can tolerate, so do whole cultures.

      (2) Cultures with a high level of uncertainty avoidance tend to value tradition and conformity.

      (3) Cultures that have a high tolerance for uncertainty and ambiguity tend to be more accepting of nonconformity and social deviance.

    d. femininity and masculinity

      (1) Femininity and masculinity influence both gender roles and the manner in which people communicate.

      (2) The degree to which a culture is masculine or feminine will influence the degree to which the culture is individualistic or collectivistic, how strong or weak the culture is with respect to uncertainty avoidance, and the degree of power distance in the culture.

B. Group diversity reflects the idea that the groups to which people belong and identify help to shape how they experience and interpret their world.

  1. Some of the groups in which people generally see themselves belonging reflect

    a. the geographic region they refer to as "home";

    b. their race and ethnicity;

    c. their gender;

    d. their religion;

    e. their socioeconomic class; and

    f. their generation.

  2. The above list does not encompass all of the types of diverse groups. Encourage students to expand this list.

C. Individual diversity makes every human being unique.

  1. Individual diversity is embedded in our personal beliefs, attitudes, and values.

    a. A belief is a conviction about whether something is true or false.

    b. Attitudes are predispositions to respond in a consistently favorable or unfavorable manner to physical and psychological objects.

    c. Values are enduring beliefs about what is good, evil, moral, and immoral.

      (1) Terminal values concern goals.

      (2) Instrumental values concern modes of conduct.

III. Rhetorical Sensitivity

A. Rhetorically sensitive people do their best to appropriately adapt their communication to the environment in which they find themselves and the diverse people who occupy it.

B. Rhetorical communicators are best understood in contrast to their two counterparts:

  1. **Noble selves** are unwavering in their belief that they must be true to their convictions. This means that they communicate what they believe, regardless of context and people.

2. **Rhetorical reflectors** are chameleon-like in their communication. They believe their messages should always be based on the ends that they hope to achieve.
C. Rhetorically sensitive people
   1. recognize the importance of being true to oneself, but also the need to consider cultural, group, and individual diversity; and
   2. understand **cultural relativism,** or the idea that admonishes people from using the criterion of appropriate behavior in their own culture to judge appropriate behavior in another culture.
D. Rhetorically sensitive people respect human complexity and avoid totalizing.
   1. **Totalizing** suggests that when we emphasize a single attribute about a person, we are in effect defining who the person is on the basis of the single attribute.
   2. The messages of rhetorically sensitive people acknowledge differences in race, ethnicity, gender, sexual orientation, and ability, but at the same time also reflect other attributes important to the identity of the person or people with whom they're communicating.
E. Rhetorically sensitive people engage in **interaction consciousness,** or try to avoid communicating in a manner that reflects only their own needs.
F. Intercultural communication scholar Benjamin J. Broome argues that, in an attempt to be rhetorically sensitive, communicators must engage in relational empathy.
   1. **Relational empathy** is concerned with the reality communicators negotiate as they communicate.
   2. To engage in relational empathy, people whose experiences are diverse should produce their own perspective, one that reflects the totality of their combined experience.

TEACHING/LEARNING OBJECTIVES

After reading Chapter 7, your students should:

- Understand the need for diversity-responsive communication.

- Be convinced that diversity is a fact of life and that to be communicatively competent one must practice diversity-responsive communication.

- Recognize the degree that culture influences the communication transaction.

- Feel less inhibited or anxious, and possibly more enthusiastic, about communicating with people from diverse cultural, social, and individual backgrounds.

- Recognize different cultural perspectives such as individualistic, collectivistic, masculine, feminine, and so on.

- Determine whether their individual communication distinguishes them as noble selves, rhetorical reflectors, or rhetorically sensitive.

- Understand the steps one must undergo to become more rhetorically sensitive and thus more communicatively competent.

- Meet the learning objectives listed on page 151 in the text.

TROUBLESHOOTING

Teaching about diversity may prove to be challenging, but the rewards will be great for both you and your students. The world we live in is becoming more diverse every day. As a result, most students and most instructors have a lot to learn. The classroom is a wonderful opportunity to practice the idea of relational empathy.

Instructors may find that some students feel reluctant to discuss either (1) their lack of knowledge about other cultures or (2) their own individual diversity resulting from their experiences, values, attitudes, and beliefs. To help overcome this potential obstacle to learning, instructors should work to create an environment that is safe. A safe environment is nonjudgmental about experiences or lack thereof and tolerant of differing points of view. Instructors' comments and behaviors should foster this environment whether they are in direct response to a student's comment or in encouragement of rhetorically sensitive comments from other classmates.

There is always the potential for disagreement. But typically by the time students reach Chapter 7 in a textbook, classrooms have developed into places where discussions and debates are relevant, respectful, and welcomed.

INSTRUCTIONAL EXERCISES

1. Ask students to describe an experience in which they realized that their culture was different from the culture they found themselves within. This experience should reflect something that surprised them. It may have to do with expectations about how things are supposed to be or how people are supposed to act. It may have to do with everyday life or with a special occasion. What is important is that the story reveals the student's conscious thoughts about what may have been their unconscious thoughts or actions. Students may discuss their intellectual, emotional, or physical responses to the situation. This exercise could become an impromptu speech, a journal entry, or a group activity. If students break into groups, have them select the most enlightening or entertaining story and ask the owner of the selected speech to represent the group and present his or her speech to the entire class. For further group involvement, have the group members help the speaker to better organize the speech by applying the guidelines for preparing effective speeches discussed in your class. This exercise might be especially interesting for foreign students but could easily include students that encountered a situation in which group or individual diversity was apparent.

2. Have students list the culture(s) and groups to which they belong. Challenge students to think about what these affiliations add to their whole being. Then, ask them to creatively demonstrate this influence to serve as a later personal reminder. This exercise aims to shed personal insight on the diverse influences that pervade students' lives. It should take only a few moments and a few lines in their notes. However, ask students if they would like to share how they see themselves. For example, some students may draw an outline of a person and indicate that their clothing is influenced by the sorority or fraternity to which they belong. They may draw a pie and show the pieces that make them whole. They may point to physical attributes and discuss where they see their origin.

3. Students are to break into groups and as a group decide on a subculture that they are familiar with that uses some common terms in very different ways than the norm. They are then to construct a list of five words with specialized or different meanings from that of the predominant culture. In a short speech, they are to define these words and explain their specialized usage. For example, computer users have a language all their own. "Ram" in normal usage is an animal, but for computer users it refers to "random access memory" in the computer. To hack something usually means to chop at it with a sharp object. For computer users, it refers to getting into other computer users' files. And while we all know what it means for a car to crash, for computer users, a crashed disc is not a physical crash so much as a failure that causes them to lose all of their data.

JOURNAL WRITING

Although diversity is prevalent, many students have little or no experience with people from different cultures, groups, or individual backgrounds. Survey your experiences to determine how you communicate with people who are dissimilar to you. Consider how you might seek additional opportunities to communicate with people from diverse cultures.

Consider your experience and determine whether the United States appears to be a masculine or feminine culture. Provide specific examples for support. How might your answer and experience differ from those of some of your classmates?

DISCUSSION TOPICS

Scott and Brydon explain that one's culture includes history, literature, music, greeting, eating, showing or not showing feelings, keeping a certain physical distance from others, making love, maintaining body hygiene, and the list goes on. Engage the class in a group discussion that describes some of the above attributes of culture as they relate to North American society. How do these cultural characteristics differ from those of other societies? Any thoughts to why we are so different (e.g., our geographic location and size vs. the closeness of European countries to their neighbors)? Are there any marked differences between East Coast and West Coast? Northern vs. southern or western vs. eastern regions of your home state? Encourage students with multicultural experiences to contribute their observations of both the United States and their native culture.

In the discussion of cultural characteristics as noted above, watch for signs of ethnocentrism. Be sure to bring these tendencies to the attention of your students in a rhetorically sensitive manner. Discuss how our egocentric views color our perceptions of dissimilar cultural practices.

TEST QUESTIONS

Multiple Choice

1. According to the authors of your text, which of the following is NOT a characteristic of individual diversity?
   *a. gender
   b. attitudes
   c. values
   d. none of the above
   Page: 153

2. According to the authors of your text, which of the following is a characteristic of group diversity?
   *a. race and ethnicity
   b. values
   c. patterns of thinking and behaving
   d. power distance
   Page: 153

3. Ethnocentric people
   a. believe their values to be morally correct.
   *b. believe their culture is superior to others.
   c. both a and b
   d. neither a nor b
   Page: 153

4. The authors of your text define *culture* as
   a. collective behaviors that people are born into.
   *b. the collective pattern of thinking, feeling, and acting characteristic of a specific human society.
   c. similarities shared among group members of a particular society.
   d. none of the above
   Page: 154

5. Culture includes the following:
   a. history
   b. literature and music
   c. eating habits
   *d. all of the above
   Page: 154

6. Culture can be described as
   a. learned.
   b. characterized by power distance.
   c. characterized by masculinity and femininity.
   *d. none of the above
   Page: 154

7. Differences in patterns of thinking, feeling, and behaving due to differences among cultures are best defined as
   a. cultural literacy.
   *b. cultural diversity.
   c. high-uncertainty-avoidance cultures.
   d. group diversity.
   Page: 154

8. All of the following are Geert Hofstede's value dimensions of culture EXCEPT
   a. collectivism and individualism.
   b. femininity and masculinity.
   *c. competitiveness and cooperativeness.
   d. none of the above
   Page: 154

9. In individualistic cultures, communication is typically
   *a. competitive.
   b. cooperative.
   c. self-serving.
   d. gender-based.
   Page: 155

10. The belief that the good of the many far outweighs the good of the few is best identified as
    a. individualism.
    b. ethnocentrism.
    *c. collectivism.
    d. patriotism.
    Page: 155

11. Power distance is
    a. the degree to which inequality exists and how it affects people.
    b. concerned with where or to whom people turn in their culture for direction.
    *c. both a and b
    d. neither a nor b
    Page: 155

12. The degree to which a culture is masculine or feminine will influence which of the following?
    a. the degree to which a culture is individualistic or collectivistic
    *b. the degree of ethnocentrism or tolerance
    c. how strong or weak the culture is with respect to uncertainty avoidance
    d. the degree of power distance
    Page: 159

13. Ethnicity is best defined as
    a. a socially defined category of people who share certain physical characteristics.
    b. differences in patterns of thinking, feeling, and behaving due to differences of individual characteristic experiences.
    *c. a cultural, national, and/or linguistic affiliation.
    d. all of the above
    Page: 164

14. Gender is all of the following EXCEPT
    a. a cultural creation.
    *b. a genetic creation.
    c. an influence on how people perceive themselves.
    d. none of the above
    Page: 165

15. _____ values concern goals. _____ values concern modes of conduct.
    a. Instrumental; Terminal
    *b. Terminal; Instrumental
    c. Individual; Terminal
    d. Individual; Instrumental
    Page: 167

16. Examples of instrumental values typically include all of the following EXCEPT
    a. ambitiousness.
    b. broad-mindedness.
    *c. a sense of accomplishment.
    d. courage.
    Page: 167

17. The statement "There is a great need for judicial reform in the United States" expresses
    *a. a belief.
    b. an attitude.
    c. a value.
    d. all of the above
    Page: 167

18. "Corporate downsizing benefits the consumer in terms of lower prices and outweighs the need to save individual jobs" expresses
    a. a belief.
    b. an attitude.
    *c. a value.
    d. all of the above
    Page: 167

19. The statement "I tend to agree with the Democratic platform" expresses
    a. a belief.
    b. an attitude.
    *c. a value.
    d. all of the above
    Page: 167

20. Cultural relativism
    *a. admonishes people from using the criteria of appropriate behavior in their own culture to judge appropriate behavior of another.
    b. recognizes that individuals have cultural, national, and linguistic affiliations that influence their perceptions.

c. is when a communicator attempts to employ the appropriate cultural norms when in a culturally diverse environment.
   d. none of the above
   Page: 168

21. Which of the following satisfy Scott and Brydon's description of the noble self?
    *a. people who communicate what they believe regardless of the context
    b. communicators who make every effort to adapt to the situation
    c. communicators who are adaptive, flexible, and appreciative of human diversity
    d. both b and c
    Page: 168

22. In the communication transaction, rhetorically sensitive people should acknowledge differences in
    a. race and ethnicity.
    b. gender and sexual orientation.
    c. abilities.
    *d. all of the above
    Page: 170

23. Self-monitoring behavior involves
    a. balancing one's needs with the needs of others.
    b. being adaptive, flexible, and appreciative of human diversity.
    *c. surveying the communication environment for cues about appropriate communication behavior.
    d. all of the above
    Page: 171

24. _____ skills require looking for cues about what constitutes appropriate communication behavior and then adapting to those cues.
    a. Flexibility and adaptiveness
    *b. Self-monitoring
    c. Cultural relativism
    d. none of the above
    Page: 173

25. _____ is the ability to see things from someone else's perspective.
    a. Sympathy
    b. Interaction consciousness
    *c. Empathy
    d. Cultural awareness
    Page: 175

True/False

26. The more dissimilar people are to us, the less accurate the attributions we make about them. (True, p. 152)

27. Attribution is the process by which we give meaning to experience. (False, p. 152)

28. Culture is an innate characteristic. (False, p. 154)

29. Cultural literacy is defined as "the understanding that one's culture includes recorded history, literature, and music." (False, p. 154)

30. Biological sex and typically gender influence the degree of collectivism or individualism upheld by cultures and their members. (True, p. 155)

31. Instructors' office hours indicate a culture with less equal power distance because students must discuss and debate issues in private. (False, p. 155)

32. Cultures with a high level of uncertainty avoidance tend to devalue tradition and conformity. (False, p. 159)

33. An ethnic group is one that is socially defined on the basis of shared physical characteristics. (False, p. 164)

34. The competent communicator focuses more energy responding to cultural diversity than individual diversity. (False, p. 167)

35. An attitude is a conviction about whether something is true or false. (False, p. 167)

36. Terminal values concern goals. (True, p. 167)

37. People's beliefs and values, but not necessarily attitudes, are tied to both their cultural heritage and the groups to which they belong. (False, p. 168)

38. Values are easier to influence and change than both beliefs and attitudes. (False, p. 167)

Short Answer/Essay

39. Explain the differences between beliefs, attitudes, and values. (p. 167)

40. Explain the statement "Diversity is essential to the well-being of us and other living things." (p. 168)

41. According to the authors of your text, people must be mindful of at least two things when traveling inside a culture other than one's own. Explain what one must to do to increase communication competence when entering a different culture. (pp. 154–159)

42. Define and explain the term *interaction consciousness*. (p. 174)

43. Explain the differences between the traditional conceptualization of empathy and that of Benjamin J. Broome's notion of relational empathy. (p.175)

CHAPTER 8
RELATIONAL COMMUNICATION

INTRODUCTION AND OUTLINE

Broadly speaking, Chapter 8 deals with relationships. Specifically, the chapter explores (1) defining relationships; (2) **relational communication;** and (3) potential **turning points** in a relationship. Main ideas discussed in Chapter 8 include:

I. Defining Relationships
   A. Relationships vary on a continuum.
      1. The quality of relationships does not automatically improve with greater intimacy.
      2. Where relationships fall on the continuum depends on the communication of the participants.
   B. The **social penetration** model, developed by psychologists Altman and Taylor, demonstrates the various relationships on the continuum by exploring the breadth (range) and depth (level of purposeful disclosure) of the messages exchanged. Following are the three levels of social penetration:
      1. **Exploratory affective exchange** exists when many topics are discussed on a relatively superficial level.
      2. **Affective exchange** exists when people are willing to chance sharing information about themselves that otherwise wouldn't be attainable.
      3. **Stable affective exchange** exists when people seem satisfied with breadth and depth of their messages and relationships.

II. Relationship Development: Initiation and Escalation
   A. Stage one: There are three variables most responsible for people **initiating** communication.
      1. **Proximity,** or physical nearness, increases the probability of initiating communication.
      2. **Perceptions of physical attraction** are the single best predictor of people initiating interaction with each other, but one must remember that perceptions of physical attraction depend on a specific culture's definition of beauty.
      3. **Perceptions of perceived similarity** suggest that the more similar we perceive a person's appearance to our own the more similar we perceive the person to us in general.
   B. Stage two: **Experimenting** involves a question-and-answer process that serves as a kind of relational filter.
      1. Experimenting involves gathering information to learn whether the other person is as similar as you believed.
      2. Experimenting allows us to filter out people we don't find socially attractive.
      3. Experimenting gives people a chance to reduce the uncertainty that is characteristic of initial encounters.
   C. Stage three: **Intensifying** involves verbally and nonverbally reminding and reinforcing the similarities between people.

      1. Intensifying signals a turning point in a relationship.
      2. What people tell each other at this point in the relationship is more spontaneous and riskier than what is communicated during the experimenting stage because it typically focuses on the people in the relationship.
  D. Stage four: **Integrating** signals that a relationship has turned in the direction of intimacy.
      1. More self-disclosure is characteristic of the integrating stage.
      2. Integrating suggests an increased level of commitment and responsibility in the relationship.
  E. Stage five: **Bonding** occurs when the verbal and nonverbal messages communicate that the relationship is a committed one.
      1. Marriage is an obvious indicator of bonding.
      2. Bonding requires willingness to give up part of your individual self in favor of one that is merged with that of the person you care about.

III. Relationship Development: Redefinition and De-escalation
  A. Stage one: **Differentiating** involves communication behaviors that focus on the dissimilarities between people.
      1. Messages begin to echo the idea that people are not as similar as they once believed.
      2. Messages sent during this stage are meant to create distance.
  B. Stage two: **Circumscribing** is designed to discourage meaningful dialogue by talking around each other.
  C. Stage three: **Stagnating** is when people are neither willing to invest the energy necessary to repair their relationship nor willing to hasten its end.
      1. They keep talk to a minimum.
      2. They talk about tasks instead of the relationship.
  D. Stage four: **Avoiding** is the last stage before the relationship is terminated.
      1. People can physically or psychologically avoid each other.
      2. Avoiding is communicated by less eye contact and touching, by sitting or standing farther apart, and by leaning away from rather than toward the person while talking.
  E. Stage five: **Terminating** a relationship can be formal (e.g., divorce) or less formal (e.g., avoiding places typically frequented by the other).
      1. People who separate physically may still be psychologically connected.
      2. Terminating may signal the end of one type of relationship and the beginning of a new kind.

IV. Managing Relational Communication
  A. There are three common goals of relational communication.
      1. Self-presentational goals concern the impression we want to create verbally and nonverbally and help us to achieve instrumental goals.
      2. Instrumental goals concern self-advancement.
      3. Relational goals indicate what is wanted from the relationship whether it be maintaining the way things are, escalation, and/or de-escalation.
  B. Regardless of the type of goal, some degree of self-disclosure is central to effective relational communication.
      1. Self-disclosure involves people purposefully exchanging information about themselves that otherwise would be unobtainable.

2. No rules govern self-disclosure behavior. It depends on the nature of the relationship and the people's personalities, goals, and levels of communication competence.
3. Three levels of self-disclosure typically characterize relational development:
   a. Level one: Topical self-disclosures are relatively neutral and risk-free.
   b. Level two: Evaluative self-disclosures are about likes and dislikes.
   c. Level three: Intimate self-disclosures are typically for close relationships because they make one vulnerable.
4. Self-disclosure plays a key role in achieving self-presentational goals and uncertainty reduction.
5. The **reciprocity norm** says that people expect their self-disclosures to be returned in kind.
6. The **Johari Window** demonstrates how a relationship changes as a result of self-disclosure.
7. On page 200, eight guidelines for making good decisions about self-disclosure appear and are more thoroughly explained.
   a. Pay attention to diversity.
   b. Think through the relationship between self-disclosure and the goals that motivate it.
   c. Avoid indiscriminate self-disclosure.
   d. Protect what is disclosed to you.
   e. Think through the consequences of a specific self-disclosure.
   f. Establish privacy boundaries.
   g. Practice reciprocity when appropriate.
   h. Be positive.
C. There are conversational skills that can help your relational communication.
   1. Skills for the relationship just being defined include following expected verbal and nonverbal conversational rules such as maintaining eye contact and employing long pauses to encourage feedback.
   2. Skills for managing conversations include recognizing the dialectic tensions of well-established relationships.
      a. Contextual dialectics require
         (1) people to understand that relationships have a private and a public dimension; and
         (2) people to balance the real with the ideal.
      b. Interactional dialectics require people to balance
         (1) independence and dependence;
         (2) affection and instrumentality;
         (3) judgment and acceptance; and
         (4) expressiveness and protectiveness.
      c. To further help manage dialectic tensions, Scott and Brydon suggest developing consensual rules for dealing with tension and displaying communication behaviors consistent with the principle of conversational coherence (which means knowing what to say, when to say it, and how to say it).
   3. Finally, conversational management of the dialectic tensions, characteristic of well-defined relationships, involves the concepts of complementarity and symmetry in relationships.

a. Complementary relational communication tells people the agree about the nature of their association.

b. Relational communication that is symmetrical is characterized by parallel messages and can be competitive or submissive.

TEACHING/LEARNING OBJECTIVES

After reading Chapter 8, students should:

- Be able to analyze their personal relational communication patterns to better understand their relationships.

- Understand relational communication patterns so as to more accurately determine the nature of other people's relationships.

- Understand and practice appropriate self-disclosure behaviors.

- Be able to explore and understand their own reasons for self-disclosure.

- Understand the models presented including the social penetration model, Knapp's relationship development model, and the Johari Window.

- Feel more confident in their ability to manage their conversations and the dialectic tensions that arise.

- Meet the learning objectives listed on page 181 in the text.

TROUBLESHOOTING

Be cautious and sensitive when discussing with students research supporting the idea that those considered more physically attractive will be a more likely target of relationally motivated communicators, as discussed on page 187. It is important to remember and stress to students that we are speaking in generalities. Students who do not fit the mold should not feel discouraged or less attractive after leaving class. Remember that decreased communication anxiety and increased communication competence are rooted in self-esteem.

INSTRUCTIONAL EXERCISES

1. When discussing Knapp's relational communication model, have students break into groups of three. Two students should quickly create a dialogue or scene that characterizes one stage of initiation or de-escalation described by Knapp's model. The third student should guess the stage being performed.

2. Divide the class into three large groups. Without allowing the members from the other groups to hear, give each group the following instructions. These instructions could be provided in writing as well.

- **Group one:** When you are joined by your group members, engage in a conversation that leads you to disclose something about yourself. Remember, self-disclosure merely involves people purposefully exchanging information about themselves that otherwise would be unobtainable. Therefore, there is no need to share your most embarrassing moment or greatest fear. Share what you feel comfortable sharing, but this kernel of information should be the primary topic that you want to talk about for the entire exercise.

- **Group two:** In the following conversations, your objective is to encourage other members of your group to talk and to continue to self-disclose information. Use all of the skills learned in Chapter 8 and throughout the class to help you achieve your goal (i.e., the reciprocity norm and nonverbal feedback).

- **Group Three:** Your role is to listen to the other group members. You are not really supposed to talk. Therefore, keep your words to the bare minimum.

After providing the directions, organize the class into teams of three which consist of one member from each of the three original groups. Inform teams that they have about 10–12 minutes and instruct them to begin. When the time has elapsed, ask students to take out a piece of paper and privately jot down three words that describe their experience and observations. Using their words as guides, engage the class in a group discussion revolving around self-disclosure and Scott and Brydon's eight guidelines for making good decisions about self-disclosure, which appear on page 200. For example, one student from group one may say "embarrassed." A discussion about what to disclose to whom and at what time can demonstrate the importance of following the guidelines of (1) avoiding indiscriminate self-disclosure and (2) thinking through the consequences of a specific self-disclosure. Another student from group two may say "obligated" because he or she may have felt unprepared to disclose at the start of the conversation but pressured because of the reciprocity norm and the other person's insistence on talking about private information. A discussion revolving around when and where it is not appropriate to practice reciprocity (guideline 7) may follow. A student from group three might feel "guilty" because he or she did not contribute anything to the conversation. This could lead to a discussion regarding how we should sometimes learn to be quiet because we often find ourselves in situations where we wish we could take back what has already been said.

JOURNAL WRITING

Reflect on the guidelines provided for making good decisions about self-disclosure. In your journal, document an instance in which you either (1) followed a guideline listed and met with success or (2) failed to follow the guidelines and think about the consequences of your communication.

Most students view the de-escalation process negatively when living through it. However, many may feel differently with hindsight. Examine past relationships that have undergone the process of redefinition and de-escalation. Describe how you felt when it was happening and how they feel about the end result now. Based on what you have now learned from Chapter 8, how could you have communicated differently, and thus more effectively, during the experience?

DISCUSSION TOPICS

If you have a multicultural class, encourage students to discuss appropriate self-disclosure behaviors from their cultures. Be careful to remember, and to delicately stress to the class, that some of the behaviors mentioned might not really be appropriate if used in North American culture, but instead might be more of a bad habit.

Using Knapp's relationship model, discuss whether or not all relationships pass through all five stages of initiation and escalation and then later redefinition and de-escalation. Ask students if they have ever had a relationship in which one or more of the stages were skipped on either the incline or decline. What was their experience? Did they feel the relationship moved too quickly or ended without warning?

TEST QUESTIONS

Multiple Choice

1. Social penetration is best defined as
   a. verbal and nonverbal messages that define the nature of the social relationship between people.
   *b. the process of exchanging messages that vary in breadth and depth.
   c. the kind of purposeful self-disclosure that adds depth to a relationship.
   d. when people seem satisfied with the number of social relationships that they are maintaining.
   Page: 182

2. Exploratory affective exchange is a theory which was developed by
   a. Mark Knapp.
   b. Steve Duck.
   *c. Irwin Altman and Dalmas Taylor.
   d. William Rawlins.
   Page: 183

3. Exploratory affective exchange is a theory which suggests that when people first get acquainted
   a. they add considerable depth to topics to discover if they would like to know one another better.
   b. they exchange messages that vary in breadth and depth.
   c. they talk about topics that are generally superficial.
   *d. both a and b
   Page: 183

4. Affective exchange signals that
   *a. people are willing to chance sharing information about themselves that otherwise would not be attainable.
   b. people seem satisfied with the characteristic breadth and depth of their messages and relationship.
   c. there has been escalation through the five stages of relationship development.
   d. none of the above
   Page: 184

5. Researchers _____ and _____ define the term *turning point* as "any event or occurrence that is associated with change in a relationship."
   a. Knapp; Erickson
   b. Altman; Taylor
   *c. Baxter; Bullis
   d. Knapp; Duck
   Page: 184

6. The social penetration model most accurately describes
   a. intimate relationships.
   b. acquaintance relationships.
   c. family relationships.
   *d. all of the above
   Page: 185

7. Knapp's model of relationship development describes which of the following steps to demonstrate how relationships potentially escalate?
   a. engaging, experimenting, integrating, trusting
   b. initiating, engaging, focusing, experimenting, bonding
   *c. initiating, experimenting, intensifying, integrating, bonding
   d. attracting, initiating, engaging, intensifying, trusting, bonding
   Page: 186

8. According to Knapp's relationship development model, which of the following promotes stage one—initiating?
   a. proximity
   b. physical attraction
   c. perceived similarity
   *d. all of the above
   Page: 186

9. According to Knapp's relationship development model, all of the following would be considered important variables as to whether or not people enter the initiating stage EXCEPT
   *a. perceived trustworthy characteristics.
   b. physical attraction.
   c. perceived similarity.
   d. proximity.
   Page: 187

10. Which stage of Knapp's relationship development model allows us to filter out people we don't find socially attractive?
    a. initiating
    *b. experimenting
    c. integrating
    d. intensifying
    Page: 188

11. In the _____ stage, people typically bring up similarities and engage in verbal and nonverbal behaviors that reinforce them.
    a. bonding
    b. integrating
    *c. intensifying
    d. experimenting
    Page: 189

12. Research indicates that often when people perceive others to be similar in terms of style of dress and age, they often perceive them to be more similar in regard to
    a. backgrounds.
    b. attitudes.
    c. values and beliefs.
    *d. all of the above
    Page: 189

13. Knapp suggests which of the following as the stages in the process of de-escalation?
    a. differentiating, stagnating, withdrawing, terminating
    b. circumscribing, stagnating, withdrawing, avoiding, terminating
    *c. differentiating, circumscribing, stagnating, avoiding, terminating
    d. differentiating, avoiding, withdrawing, terminating
    Page: 192

14. Self-disclosure is all of the following EXCEPT
    *a. a crucial stage in Knapp's relationship development model.
    b. the process of purposefully exchanging information about oneself that would otherwise be unobtainable.
    c. topical, evaluative, and intimate.
    d. none of the above
    Page: 197

15. The Johari Window is designed to
    a. demonstrate the concept that when people give something to someone they expect something in return.
    b. describe the process by which people purposefully reveal information about themselves that would otherwise be unobtainable.
    *c. show what is known, unknown, and hidden between people.
    d. all of the above
    Page: 199

16. The idea that people expect their self-disclosures to be returned in kind is known by researchers as the
    a. self-disclosure norm.
    *b. reciprocity norm.
    c. equal disclosure norm.
    d. Johari norm.
    Page: 199

17. All of the following are guidelines for making good decisions about self-disclosure EXCEPT
    a. avoiding indiscriminate self-disclosure.
    *b. eliminating privacy boundaries in well-defined relationships.
    c. practicing reciprocity when appropriate.
    d. being positive.
    Page: 199

18. Conversational management involves
    *a. understanding conversational rules.
    b. adhering to the reciprocity norm.
    c. exchanging personal insights.
    d. none of the above
    Page: 202

19. Relational dialectics are best described as
    *a. the contextual and interactional tensions that are inherent in relationships.
    b. the verbal and nonverbal rules that govern talk in the process of relational definition.
    c. the widely documented principles that demonstrate people give something because they expect something in return.
    d. none of the above
    Page: 204

20. According to Rawlins, which of the following are the two contextual dialectics people need to manage communicatively to help lessen tension?
    *a. (1) the real versus the ideal and (2) the public and private dimension
    b. (1) the intimate versus professional and (2) the public versus personal
    c. (1) the real versus imagined and (2) the private versus the presented self
    d. (1) the expressive and (2) the protective
    Page: 204

True/False

21. Since relationships vary on a continuum, we can have satisfying relationships anywhere along the continuum. (True, p. 182)

22. The quality of our relationships automatically gets better as we become more intimate. (False, p. 190)

23. Intimate people speak less formally to one another than acquaintances. (True, p. 190)

24. Mark Knapp constructed the social penetration model to demonstrate the breadth and depth of messages exchanged. (False, pp. 184–187)

25. When people first meet, they are likely to include more depth of topics than breadth of topics in their conversations. (False, p. 183)

26. The process of engaging in a conversation covering a wide range of topics is defined by Altman and Taylor as exploratory affective exchange. (True, p. 183)

27. Affective exchange signals to the competent communicator that those involved in the communication transaction are willing to chance self-disclosing. (True, p. 184)

28. Self-disclosing signals that the relationship has reached a potential turning point. (True, pp. 197–199)

29. Self-disclosure inevitably leads to greater commitment in nonromantic relationships. (False, p. 199)

30. Affective exchange explains the point in a relationship when all parties agree that the breadth and depth of the messages exchanged are positively impacting the relationship development process. (False, p. 184)

31. Stable affectiveness can occur at any level of social penetration. (True, p. 184)

32. Proximity is a critical component of the experimenting stage of Knapp's relationship development model. (False, pp. 186–187)

33. Because North America is such a heterogeneous population, there is little consensus regarding the standards for physical beauty. (False, p. 187)

34. Research indicates that physical attraction is still the single best predictor of two people initiating interaction with each other. (True, p. 187)

35. The more similar we perceive a person's appearance to our own, the more similar we perceive the person to us in general. (True, p. 188)

36. Social attraction is largely based on how skillfully people communicate. (True, p. 188)

37. In the integrating stage of the relationship development process, people are less likely to share information about their pasts than they would in the intensifying stage. (False, p. 190)

38. As defined by Knapp, bonding requires communication competence and psychological maturity. (True, p. 190)

39. The process of de-escalation can be described as redefining the relationship. (True, p. 191)

40. When relationships are just initiating, the norm in North America is that people need to be especially careful not to engage in more personal types of self-disclosure (True, p. 198)

41. Self-disclosures should be reciprocal among people during their initial encounters. (True, p. 199)

42. Complementary relational communication is characterized by parallel messages. (False, p. 207)

43. Symmetrical messages are characterized as being primarily competitive. (False, p. 208)

Short Answer/Essay

44. Explain some of the conditions and factors discussed in Chapter 8, which may determine whether a relationship thrives or dies. (pp. 186–190)

45. List two relational communication clues that indicate that communicators are intimate, not merely acquaintances. (p. 190)

46. Explain the statement that relationships vary on a continuum. (p. 182)

47. List and explain the relationship among the stages of Knapp's relationship development model. (pp. 186–187)

48. Explain the characteristics of a relationship when it reaches the point of *stable affective exchange*. (pp. 184–185)

49. Explain the Johari Window and how it received its name. (p. 200)

50. Explain the differences between Rawlins's contextual and interactional dialectics. (pp. 203–204)

CHAPTER 9
FAMILY COMMUNICATION

INTRODUCTION AND OUTLINE

In Chapter 9 students learn about one of the most significant dimensions of communication in which they participate. Understanding family communication is essential to becoming a competent communicator because our families shape first how we see ourselves and then how we relate to others. Chapter 9 clearly demonstrates to students how all families are both alike and unique. More specifically, Scott and Brydon cover the following material:

I. The family system
   A. A family is a system of relational communication whose members perform interdependent roles, are bound by history or choice, and create a collective memory through storytelling, themes, and myths.
   B. Recall from Chapter 1 that a system is a collection of interdependent parts arrayed in such a way that a change in one will effect changes in all others.
   C. Five common family types
      1. **Open family systems** encourage members to interact with people outside the family and then readily adapt to the inputs that result from those exchanges.
      2. **Closed family systems** discourage outside interaction because the heads of closed family systems, which are hierarchical by nature, see little to be gained from these exchanges.
      3. **Random family systems** have ambiguous boundaries and rules, and members face unpredictability.
      4. **Enmeshed family systems** strive for cohesiveness and are neither completely opened nor completely closed.
      5. **Disengaged family systems** reinforce extreme individualism.
   D. Family attributes
      1. **Family size and members' roles** influence the family system.
         a. Potentially more intimate and accurate communication results from fewer lines of communication.
         b. According to scholar Erving Goffman, a role is a pattern of behavior in which a family member is expected to routinely engage.
         (1) Regardless of size, members each have one or more roles.
         (2) Galvin and Brommel list five essential family role functions:
            (a) providing for adult sexual fulfillment and gender modeling for children;
            (b) providing nurturing and emotional support;
            (c) providing for individual development;
            (d) providing kinship maintenance and family management; and
            (e) providing basic resources.

2. **Inputs and outputs** influence the family system.
    a. Inputs are messages a family receives from sources outside the system.
    b. Family systems produce outputs which influence how family members see themselves and the subsystems surrounding them.
3. **Boundaries and hierarchies** characterize the family system.
    a. Boundaries define who belongs to the family and who doesn't.
    b. Hierarchies define who possesses influence and the power to make decisions in the family.
4. **Rules** govern the family system. Rules may be explicit, implicit, arbitrary, or consensually developed.
5. The **goals** of the family system are reflected in the communication behaviors of the family members.
6. Family communication systems feature **feedback mechanisms** intended to regulate the interdependent behaviors of individual family members.

II. Networks and subsystems
   A. A network is composed of the links that connect the lines of communication in a family system.
   B. Subsystems are characterized by the same features that appear in larger systems (i.e., roles, rules, and feedback mechanisms).
   C. Internal and external networks and subsystems tell us about the flow of communication and the degree of hierarchy inside a system.
      1. Internal networks focus on the family members and their relationships to one another.
      2. External networks and subsystems that influence the system include outside forces such as work and the government.

III. Family storytelling
   A. Not only does your family constitute a culture in its own right, your family experience provides you with a sense of the larger culture and your beliefs about appropriate communication behavior relative to it.
   B. The cultural lessons we learn from our families are part of a larger story that families pass along from generation to generation.
   C. Family stories constitute relational communication.
      1. Stories teach lessons and establish boundaries of right and wrong.
      2. Stories also help to connect one generation to another; create a collective memory among family members; and shape family identity.
   D. Like any other story that has been told and retold, the narratives that describe a family's history reflect certain themes and myths.
      1. A theme is an idea that is threaded throughout many family stories (e.g., personal sacrifice and struggle).
      2. According to family communication scholars, myths can serve to assist families in
         a. maintaining important attitudes, beliefs, and values;
         b. managing role conflicts;
         c. reinforcing generational bonds; and
         d. coping with emotional duress.

IV. Family roles and functions
   A. Communication researcher Mary Anne Fitzpatrick identified four types of **spousal roles:**
      1. Traditional couples' roles are likely to be differentiated yet complementary.
         a. Men perform largely instrumental roles like earning the income and paying the bills.
         b. Women perform more expressive roles like emotionally supporting their husbands and taking care of the children and home.
         c. Fitzpatrick considers these roles differentiated and complementary because traditional couples believe that one's gender dictates what roles they are best-suited for.
      2. Independent couples continuously negotiate their roles and tend to cross the gender lines that, for traditional couples, define responsibilities.
      3. Separate couples enjoy considerable independence but divide roles more traditionally.
      4. Mixed couples have mismatched perceptions of their relationship and role expectations.
   B. The role of parent in a family is multifunctional.
      1. The role of parent involves nurturing, encouraging and assuring, socializing, disciplining, and so forth.
      2. The multifunctional parent role proves challenging because the functions that parents are expected to perform may often be at odds with each other.
   C. Role conflicts often occur between parental and spousal roles or between a woman who is expected to perform instrumental roles and all the expressive roles as well.

V. Dialectic tensions in families
   A. Scott and Brydon cite several excellent movie examples to help students understand dialectic tensions in Chapter 9. If needed, refer students to the additional discussion of dialectic tensions in Chapter 8.
   B. Dialectic tensions fall into two general categories:
      1. Contextual dialectics reflect the subsystem and networks surrounding the family in relation to the tension between (1) the private vs. public image presented and (2) the real vs. ideal expectations.
      2. Interactional dialectics reflect the relational communication that defines and redefines the nature of the association among family members.
         a. Four interactional dialectics can cause relational tension:
            (1) independence vs. dependence;
            (2) affection and instrumentality;
            (3) judgment and acceptance; and
            (4) expressiveness and protectiveness.
         b. Scott/Brydon cite specific examples to describe the above tensions.
   C. The dialectic of change in the family system
      1. Even though change is a constant in family life, it also is a source of dialectic tension in families.
      2. Research shows that people tend to resist change even when change appears in their best interests.
      3. Family researchers David Olson and Hamilton McCubbin report seven stages in the development of the heterosexual family.

a. Stage one involves married couples without children.

b. Stage two involves married couples with preschool-age children.

c. Stage three involves married couples with school-age children.

d. Stage four involves families with adolescents.

e. Stage five involves families with children entering adulthood.

f. Stages six and seven refer to the empty nest and retirement years.

D. Family communication skills

1. The principles for regulating conversation in close relationships discussed in Chapter 8 apply to family communication as well as the following skills.

2. Every family system is different. Thus, the effectiveness of the following communication skills varies from family to family.

3. Accepting **ownership** of our communication and its potential consequences involves the following:

a. Identify the content and intent of messages as yours.

b. Communication scholars Noller and Fitzpatrick suggest that we use more "I" messages.

c. Ownership and "I" statements help families manage dialectic tensions because:

(1) Ownership requires family members to be mindful of the consequences that may result from expressing a feeling or belief.

(2) "I" messages acknowledge that the feeling or belief belongs to the speaker.

(3) "I" messages are not accusatory in meaning and therefore will less likely be met with a defensive response.

d. **Documenting** requires that family members provide specific evidence to support a claim.

e. Families should **protect self-esteem** and therefore should always consider the potential of a message to negatively and unfairly detract from another member's self-esteem.

f. A family member's inability to listen is a common complaint from spouses and children. **Listen actively.**

g. Effective family communication requires practicing **rhetorically sensitive** communication.

TEACHING/LEARNING OBJECTIVES

After reading Chapter 9, your students should:

- Understand the concept of a system and why a family constitutes one.

- Identify their individual family type and roles within that system.

- Practice communication skills associated with effective family communication.

- Identify family stories, themes, and myths and the purposes they serve.

- Meet the learning objectives listed on page 213 in the text.

TROUBLESHOOTING

When discussing effective and ineffective family communication, keep in mind that you will indirectly be evaluating some of the most important people in your students' lives. With this in mind, use rhetorically sensitive, nonjudgmental language in all discussions.

INSTRUCTIONAL EXERCISES

Children and parents inevitably experience conflict. One cause may be the fact that the role of parenting is multifunctional and that often the individual roles are at odds with one another. Have students in groups of two come up with and share personal experiences in which at the time of conflict they failed to see the dilemma that faced their parents. For this exercise, allow students to select their partner and encourage them to work with someone they are comfortable with.

JOURNAL WRITING

In Chapter 9, Scott and Brydon discuss the role of stories, themes, and myths in the family communication system. Reflect on your family and your upbringing. What stories, themes, and myths have been part of your family experience? What purposes did they serve?

DISCUSSION TOPICS

Democrats and Republicans alike discuss the breakdown of the family and its impact on society in many of their political speeches. Do you agree with these statements? If so, what role does ineffective communication in any given individual family play in shaping society as a whole?

On page 215, Scott and Brydon explain that every family system is different, and thus the effectiveness of the communication skills outlined in the chapter will vary. As a way to explore differences in families and levels of effectiveness, in a positive and optimistic way, ask students to reflect on what Scott and Brydon's statements mean to them individually.

TEST QUESTIONS

Multiple Choice

1. Random family systems are characterized as
    a. adaptable.
  *b. ambiguous.
    c. neither completely open nor completely closed.
    d. rigid.
    Page: 215

2. Open family systems
    a. encourage extensive communication among family members but discourage involving people outside the family in what are considered family matters.
  *b. welcome family members interacting with people outside the family and encourage them to do so.

c. use open communication among family members to achieve their primary goal of family cohesiveness.

d. Operate within ambiguous boundaries.

Page: 215

3. The authors of your text define *family* by all of the following characteristics EXCEPT

*a. members performing independent roles.

b. members being bound by history.

c. members being potentially bound by choice.

d. members sharing a collective memory.

Page: 215

4. The disengaged family system

a. discourages family members from interacting with people outside the family.

*b. reinforces extreme individualism.

c. requires members to sacrifice their independence.

d. all of the above

Page: 216

5. According to the authors of your text, which of the following is NOT a characteristic of families?

a. established boundaries about who belongs in the family

b. assigned roles that members are expected to perform

c. rules that govern family life

*d. none of the above

Page: 216

6. All of the following are essential family role functions EXCEPT

a. providing adult sexual fulfillment.

*b. providing pleasure and entertainment for children.

c. providing gender modeling for children.

d. providing emotional support.

Page: 216

7. Family roles may include which of the following?

a. family achiever

b. family clown

c. family scapegoat

*d. all of the above

Page: 216

8. _____ are messages a family receives from sources outside the system.

a. Contextual dialectics

*b. Inputs

c. Interactional dialectics

d. Outputs

Page: 217

9. Canonical stories
    a. help connect one generation to the another.
   *b. relay what is considered to be appropriate behavior.
    c. create a collective memory.
    d. detail pivotal and seemingly miraculous events in a family's history.
    Page: 221

10. Subsystems can be either complementary meaning _____ or symmetrical meaning _____.
    a. cohesive; similar
    b. flexible; hierarchical
   *c. cooperative; competitive
    d. masculine; feminine
    Page: 221

11. A subsystem is characterized by all of the following EXCEPT
    a. members having roles and rules.
   *b. members contributing to meeting the basic needs.
    c. members giving feedback.
    d. none of the above
    Page: 221

12. The authors of your text list all of the following as family communication skills EXCEPT
    a. listening actively.
    b. pinpointing.
   *c. using "we" statements.
    d. documenting.
    Page: 222

13. According to the authors of your text, myths can serve to assist families in all of the following functions EXCEPT
    a. managing role conflicts.
    b. reinforcing generational bonds.
   *c. building and protecting self-esteem.
    d. maintaining values.
    Page: 224

14. Regardless of family size, families will
    a. experience change.
    b. have boundaries and hierarchies.
    c. produce outputs.
   *d. all of the above
    Pages: 216–219

15. Independent couples will typically
    a. accomplish individual tasks divided according to gender.
    b. have men fulfilling instrumental roles and women performing expressive roles.
   *c. continuously negotiate their roles.
    d. have different perceptions of their relationship and different role expectations.
    Page: 227

16. Which of the following is NOT an interactional dialectic?
    *a. cooperation and competition
    b. independence and dependence
    c. judgment and acceptance
    d. none of the above
    Page: 232

17. The empty-nest couple is characterized as one
    a. that needs to discover topics in common other than their children.
    b. that has grown children who have left home.
    *c. both a and b
    d. neither a nor b
    Page: 234

18. Which of the following is NOT an encouraged family communication skill?
    a. expressing ownership
    b. protecting self-esteem
    c. listening actively
    *d. none of the above
    Page: 235

19. The family communication skill "documenting" refers to
    a. incorporating "I" statements to take responsibility for your messages.
    *b. providing specific evidence to support a claim.
    c. both a and b
    d. neither a nor b
    Page: 236

20. Effective family communication is which of the following?
    a. rhetorically sensitive
    b. based on recognition of the family system's complexity
    c. adaptive to changes in the family system
    *d. all of the above
    Page: 237

True/False

21. Closed family systems integrate input from exchanges between the heads of the household and people from outside the family. (False, p. 215)

22. Random family systems strive for cohesiveness using a variety of techniques. (False, p. 215)

23. The enmeshed system is the most collectivistic of the five common family types. (True, p. 215)

24. In every family, regardless of type or size, members have roles. (True, p. 216)

25. It is likely that in any one family, any one member can have several roles. (True, p. 216)

26. Outputs are messages received from members outside the family system. (False, p. 217)

27. Symmetrical subsystems are cooperative. (False, p. 221)

28. Instrumental roles are characterized by activities such as taking care of the home and children. (False, p. 227)

29. Although people tend to resist change, even when it's in their best interest, change in a relationship is inevitable. (True, p. 234)

30. Communication scholars Patricia Noller and Mary Anne Fitzpatrick suggest that families incorporate more "we" statements into their communication because people intuitively recognize that the plural pronoun "we" potentially carries more weight with people than the singular pronoun "I." (False, p. 235)

31. The communication skill of documenting is often referred to as pinpointing. (True, p. 236)

Short Answer/Essay

32. The authors of your text state that all families are alike and yet unique. List and explain what families share and what factors make them unique. (p. 216)

33. List the five essential family role functions that researchers have identified, according to authors Kathleen Galvin and Bernard Brommel. (p. 216)

34. Explain the empty-nest syndrome. (p. 234)

35. What is the role of storytelling in the family system? (p. 222)

CHAPTER 10
RELATIONAL CONFLICT

INTRODUCTION AND OUTLINE

Despite public opinion, conflict is not abnormal and need not be destructive. In fact, conflict is inevitable in relationships and can be constructive. Managing relational conflict requires both knowledge and skill—the subjects covered in Chapter 10.

I. The nature or conflict
   A. Misconceptions about conflict include:
      1. Conflict is abnormal.
      2. Conflict is always destructive.
      3. Conflict results from communication breakdown.
      4. Conflict should be resolved as quickly as possible.
   B. What is conflict?
      1. Conflict involves interdependent relationships.
      2. Conflict begins with interdependent parties perceiving things differently.
      3. Conflict exists when people perceive
         a. they can't get what they want if others get what they want;
         b. whatever it is that they want; there is not enough to share equally; and
         c. even when people do want the same thing, someone or some agency is preventing them from getting it.
   C. Types of conflicts
      1. Destructive conflict most often involves people verbally and nonverbally abusing each other.
         a. It is typically characterized by an escalatory spiral—a visual depiction of how unmanaged conflict intensifies with time.
         b. It is often motivated by the desire to make the other person suffer.
      2. Constructive conflict involves change.
         a. It demands people be flexible.
         b. It assists people in learning about each other and the issues at hand.
         c. It should enhance not diminish self-esteem.
   D. Common sources of relational conflict
      1. **Perceptual bias.** Seeing things from a particular point of view based on experiences or lack thereof may cause relational conflict.
      2. **Interdependence.** In a relationship, there is no such thing as hurting only yourself.
      3. **Goals.** When one person's behavior is perceived as inconsistent with the realization of another person's unstated goals, relational conflict is probable.
      4. **Scarce resources.** When there is too little of what is perceived as needed in the relationship, conflicts often arise.
      5. **Outside interference.** Perceived interference from a party outside the relationship often causes relational conflict.

II. Communication and conflict
  A. Conflict management begins with an analysis of the relationship between communication behavior and the perceptual struggles we experience over goals, resources, and outside interference. This kind of analysis involves learning about our conflict style and the customary message strategies we use under conditions of conflict.
  B. Conflict styles
    1. Your conflict style is a pattern of communication behavior you are likely to exhibit when confronted with a potential struggle over goals, resources, or outside influence.
      a. A style is something to which you are predisposed.
      b. Research indicates we believe ourselves to be people who resolve conflict in a positive way while perceiving others as doing just the opposite.
      c. Five common conflict styles include:
        (1) **Avoidance** represents people who go out of their way to escape conflict.
        (2) **Collaboration** means people working together to find a mutually discovered solution.
        (3) **Competition** produces a winner even if winning comes at the expense of others.
        (4) **Compromise** involves giving something up in order to gain something else.
        (5) **Accommodation** involves indulging or adapting to the needs of the others.
    2. People rarely use the same style of conflict in all situations.
  C. Message strategies
    1. A message strategy serves as a plan or framework that people use to guide the communication behavior during conflict.
    2. People tend to engage in two distinct message strategies.
      a. **Integrative** message strategies are prosocial and collaborative and approach conflict as a win-win situation.
      b. **Distributive** message strategies are antisocial and controlling and treat conflict as a win-lose situation.

III. Constructive conflict management
  A. The constructive management of conflict is part knowledge (of what to do and not to do) and part skill.
  B. Conflict management skills suggest people:
    1. Consider others.
      a. Engage in integrative vs. distributive message strategies.
      b. Use specific techniques to show the other person your concern for his or her well-being.
        (1) Listen actively to the other person.
        (2) Validate the person's self-worth.
        (3) Be consistent with your verbal and nonverbal messages.
        (4) Don't patronize the other person.
        (5) Don't interrupt.

2. Keep emotions in check and arguments rational. Strategies include:
   a. Avoid distributive messages.
   b. Learn to distinguish among messages that are assertive, argumentative, and hostile.
      (1) Assertive messages tend to establish leadership and control of the situation.
      (2) Argumentative messages strive to defend people's rights and interests.
      (3) Hostile messages aim to protect a feeling or belief.
   c. Don't catastrophize, or make things look worse than what they really are.
   d. Avoid trying to "one up" hostile messages.
   e. Mind your meta-message and try not to intensify the emotions you feel nonverbally.
   f. Take control of your anger.
3. Express yourself precisely.
   a. Be specific.
   b. Avoid generalizations.
   c. Use "I" messages.
   d. Be descriptive.
   e. Stay focused and in the moment.
4. Bring the conflict to resolution.
   a. Establish a time to talk about the conflict and feelings associated with it.
   b. Clarify the issues.
   c. Be open.
   d. Take time to find long-term solutions.
   e. Accentuate the positive.
5. Accentuate the positive.
   a. Be immediate. Increase your perceptions of openness.
   b. Be encouraging.
   c. Relieve tension.

TEACHING/LEARNING OBJECTIVES

After reading Chapter 10, your students should:

- Recognize that conflict is a central feature of relational life and therefore needs to be better understood.

- Determine if they tend to believe any of the common misconceptions about conflict.

- Feel more confident that engaging in constructive conflict vs. destructive conflict can actually strengthen the relationship.

- Recognize the five common sources of conflict in relationships.

- Understand the need to approach conflict and how to approach it with integrative message strategies vs. distributive message strategies.

- Identify and practice the skills that help to constructively manage conflict.

- Set constructive conflict management goals for future experiences.

- Meet the learning objectives listed on page 243 in the text.

TROUBLESHOOTING

In a class that incorporates small group exercises, the potential for conflict is great. This is especially the case when individual grades hinge on group performance. Part of the small group learning experience includes managing conflict, and as a result instructors need to resist the temptation to intervene in group affairs whenever possible. However, instructors also need to recognize instances in which some guidance is necessary. Chapter 10 discusses how unstated and incompatible goals are a source of conflict. Be aware that students who take the class pass/fail or credit/no credit will probably have different goals from those students who are taking the class for a grade.

When teaching about conflict, keep in mind what Scott and Brydon point out on p. 244. Research indicates that most of us perceive ourselves as conflict resolvers who accomplish this task through positive methods, while we view others as the exact opposite. As a result, in any conflict-resolution exercises where either you or your students point out destructive communication patterns, there is the potential for disagreement, distrust of the material, excuses and exceptions, and disappointment in one's individual behaviors. When talking about conflict, it is important to make sure the classroom environment is open and supportive.

INSTRUCTIONAL EXERCISES

1. At the end of one class period, have groups of two students create a conflict scenario and write out the details to be collected by you. In the time between class periods, have the scenarios created into handouts. This can be as simple as inputting the material into the computer, possibly adjusting the scenarios to add to the overall discussions of the conflict, and making a few copies. You can use all of the scenarios or select the best ones. In a subsequent class period, direct students to break into different groups of two. Give each group a conflict and ask them to discuss how they would approach the conflict using the principles discussed in Chapter 10. Ask students to be specific in regard to conflict styles, message strategies, and the skills they would employ to constructively manage the conflict they are facing. In 2–3-minute speeches, have one partner explain the scenario and the other explain his or her approach. Instructors may also choose to create their own scenarios for time-saving purposes. However, keep in mind that students are more interested and therefore will listen more attentively if they are involved in the entire process of the exercise. To further ensure total class involvement, after each speech ask the authors of the scenario how they feel about the suggested approach. What would they suggest be done differently? Find out if the scenario they created was based on their life experiences.

2. Organize students into five groups. Assign each group one of the conflict styles: (1) avoidance, (2) collaboration, (3) competition, (4) compromise, or (5) accommodation. Direct students to script a 2–3-minute role-play scenario that reflects the conflict style assigned to them. Encourage them to include verbal as well as nonverbal messages. But instruct them that they must never explicitly state the style they are depicting. Have the students not involved in the role-playing take a group "quiz" to rank the effectiveness of the role players. After each scenario, have students

vote whether they believe the scenario depicted (1) avoidance, (2) collaboration, (3) competition, (4) compromise, or (5) accommodation. Keep score on the board. Provide some incentive to the group that clearly depicted their conflict style to the most students.

JOURNAL WRITING

Describe a conflict situation in which you wished things had worked out differently. Consider your part and the other person's contributions to the end result. Based on what you learned in Chapter 10, has your original opinion of yourself and your behavior changed in regard to how you handled this particular situation?

Is there a relationship that has dissolved as a result of a past conflict that was not managed effectively? Consider what skills you may now have or what action you might be able to take to resolve this conflict. Ponder whether or not this is something worth pursuing.

DISCUSSION TOPICS

In Chapter 10, we learn about the conflict style of competition and its many disadvantages. Discuss the connotations that surround the word *competition* in different types of relationships. For instance, is competition viewed differently in one's intimate relationships than in one's professional relationships? How about in small groups? In public or mass communication settings? In family communication? Explore the idea that although competition has many disadvantages, it may also have advantages for the competent communicator.

TEST QUESTIONS

Multiple Choice

1. Which statements are NOT common misconceptions about conflict?
    a. Conflict should be resolved as quickly as possible.
    b. Conflict results from communication breakdown.
    c. Conflict is always destructive.
    *d. none of the above
    Page: 245

2. Conflict can be a result of
    a. perceptions of scare resources.
    b. perceptions of incompatible goals.
    c. interference from others.
    *d. all of the above
    Page: 246

3. According to Chapter 10, types of conflict include
   *a. destructive and constructive.
   b. real and perceived.
   c. descriptive and evaluative.
   d. verbal and nonverbal.
   Page: 246

4. Common sources of relational conflict include
   a. goals.
   b. scarce resources.
   c. similar experiences.
   *d. both a and b
   Page: 246

5. When teenagers and their parents experience role conflict, they are encountering which source of relational conflict?
   a. goals
   *b. interdependence
   c. perceptual balance
   d. outside interference
   Page: 246

6. Destructive conflict is typically characterized by
   a. an escalatory spiral.
   b. aiming to make the other person suffer.
   c. verbal and nonverbal abuse.
   *d. all of the above
   Page: 247

7. Which of the following is NOT a common source of relational conflict?
   a. perceptual bias
   b. interdependence
   *c. independence
   d. outside interference
   Page: 248

8. Perceptual bias can be explained as
   a. a common source of relational conflict.
   b. commonly the result of ethnocentrism.
   c. conflict over unstated goals.
   *d. both a and b
   Page: 248

9. Which of the following is NOT a common conflict style?
   a. avoidance
   *b. confrontation
   c. compromise
   d. collaboration
   Page: 250

10. All of the following are conflict styles EXCEPT
    a. compromise.
    b. competition.
    *c. confrontation.
    d. avoidance.
    Page: 252

11. Paul and Mary are deciding which movie they should see on their Friday night date. Mary really wants to see the newest action-adventure film, and Paul is in the mood for a drama. After much discussion, Mary decides Paul can decide since it is his turn to pay for the date. Mary is approaching this conflict situation with which of the following conflict styles?
    a. collaboration
    b. compromise
    *c. accommodation
    d. avoidance
    Page: 252

12. The term used to describe a technique to enhance one's own position during and following a conflict is
    a. situative strategy.
    *b. distributive strategy.
    c. escalatory spiral.
    d. integrative strategy.
    Page: 254

13. Distributive message strategies reflect
    a. the integrated efforts to find a long-term solution that satisfies all involved.
    *b. the desire to win at the expense of the other person losing.
    c. cooperative and competitive efforts that are at odds with each other.
    d. none of the above
    Page: 254

14. An antisocial and controlling message strategy designed to enhance one's own position during and following a conflict is best defined as
    a. an integrative strategy.
    b. a distancing strategy.
    *c. a distributive strategy.
    d. none of the above
    Page: 254

15. Integrative message styles
    *a. are prosocial.
    b. treat conflict as a situation in which there must be a winner and a loser in the system.
    c. aim to allow one person to gain control of the situation.
    d. Incorporate numerous methods for gaining control of a situation.
    Page: 254

16. To constructively manage conflict, the authors of the text suggest
    *a. being specific and descriptive.
    b. using "we" messages.
    c. evaluating issues with "you" messages.
    d. both a and b
    Page: 256

17. Specific communication behaviors that contribute to destructive conflict include all of the following EXCEPT
    a. treating conflict as a win-lose situation.
    b. catastrophizing messages.
    *c. distinguishing among assertive, argumentative, and hostile messages.
    d. responding to all assertive messages similarly.
    Page: 258

18. The difference between assertive and argumentative messages is that
    a. assertive messages are aggressive but not hostile.
    *b. argumentative messages offer evidence or support for an assertion.
    c. both a and b
    d. neither a nor b
    Page: 259

19. To constructively manage conflict, Scott and Brydon suggest speaking precisely. This behavior involves all of the following EXCEPT
    a. staying focused in the moment.
    b. using "I" messages.
    c. being descriptive.
    *d. none of the above
    Page: 260

20. Constructive management conflict requires all of the following EXCEPT
    a. considering the other.
    b. accentuating the positive.
    *c. quickly moving toward a resolution.
    d. clarifying the issues.
    Page: 261

True/False

21. Conflict is normal and often even necessary. (True, p. 244)

22. Interpersonal conflict is a regular feature in even the most healthy relationships. (True, p. 244)

23. Due to its nature, conflict typically produces nothing of value in a relationship. (False, p. 245)

24. Since conflict has so many potential disadvantages, it should be avoided whenever possible. (False, p. 246)

25. Constructive conflict is characterized by the escalatory spiral. (False, p. 247)

26. People tend to use the same conflict style in all types of conflict situations they experience on a daily basis. (False, p. 250)

27. Collaboration involves each person giving something up for the other person in order to gain something back from that person. (False, p. 250)

28. Distributive message strategies are collaborative. (False, p. 254)

Short Answer/Essay

29. Explain conflict and when it typically exists. (pp. 246–247)

30. Explain why the authors of your text believe that compromise often looks better than it actually proves to be. (p. 253)

31. Identify and discuss the different conflict styles. Are one or more styles more effective or appropriate than the others? (p. 250)

32. Define the two types of message strategies. (p. 254)

33. As discussed in Chapter 10, list and explain the five skills which help to constructively manage conflict. (pp. 256–257)

CHAPTER 11
INTERVIEWING

INTRODUCTION AND OUTLINE

Chapter 11 covers the three common types of interviews and the responsibilities of both the interviewer and the interviewee before, during, and after the interview. Scott and Brydon provide practical suggestions to help students get the information they need, the job they desire, and the most from their performance appraisals. Specifically, they discuss:

I. The information-gathering interview
   A. Before the interview be sure to:
      1. Contact the potential interviewee well in advance.
      2. Do some general reading on the topic.
      3. Prepare specific questions in advance.
   B. During the interview be sure to:
      1. Show up on time, dressed professionally, and be ready to begin.
      2. Begin with general questions.
      3. Ask for leads.
      4. Listen effectively.
      5. Take notes.
      6. Ask for additional information.
      7. Say thanks.
   C. After the interview be sure to:
      1. Follow up.
      2. Transcribe notes.
      3. Follow leads.
      4. Build credibility by informing your audience that you spoke with an expert.

II. The employment interview
   A. Interviewers responsibilities
      1. Adequate preparation is essential to conducting a good interview.
         a. Familiarize yourself with the requirements of the Equal Employment Opportunity (EEO) laws and the American Disabilities Act.
            (1) The key to complying with these laws is that you ask potential employees only questions related to bona fide occupational qualifications.
            (2) Employers may ask questions regarding education, work experience, skills, and the like. They cannot legally ask questions about age, marital status, race, religion, ethnicity, disability, and the like.
         b. Develop a clear set of criteria for the position being filled.
         c. Develop a preliminary set of questions to ask candidates.
            (1) This strategy will lead to a more focused interview.
            (2) This will help to protect you against potential charges of discrimination.
         d. Familiarize yourself with the applicant's résumé.

2. Conducting the interview
   a. It is important to always act professional and courteous when conducting an interview.
   b. Just like a speech or paper, an interview has an opening, body, and close.
      (1) The **opening** includes the greeting, handshake, and small talk with the applicant. It also involves ensuring the applicant's comfort. Too much small talk can make the applicant uncomfortable.
      (2) The **body** should begin with a preview of how the interview will be organized. When organizing the interview, keep in mind:
         (a) It is good to begin with open-ended, relatively easy questions which will help to relax the applicant and get the maximum amount of information immediately.
            i. The "inverted funnel" is asking closed-ended questions first and then later open-ended questions.
            ii. Research shows many interviewers make their decision within the first four minutes of the interview.
         (b) Interviewers should avoid certain types of questions.
            i. Yes/No questions give the interviewee little opportunity to provide information.
            ii. Double-barreled questions combine two answers in one.
            iii. Leading questions convey to the interviewee how you want him or her to answer.
            iv. Guessing-game questions occur when the interviewer guesses at the answer and asks the interviewee if that is correct.
            v. Evaluative-response questions reveal the interviewer's feelings about a prospective answer.
            vi. Illegal questions such as those which violate the EEO laws or ADA are obviously not recommended.
            vii. Yes-response questions are not insightful.
            viii. Résumé questions are pointless since they repeat information already provided.
         (c) More effective questions to ask revolve around areas such as interest in the organization; general or specific work-related topics; education and training; career path and goals; previous job performance; salary and benefits; and the career field in general.
         (d) It is often important to provide the interviewee with information about the organization and position.
         (e) Provide an opportunity for the interviewee to ask questions.
      (3) In the **close** the interviewer should explain what will happen next. Tell the applicant if there are organizational procedures that need to be attended, if there will be additional interview opportunities, and when he or she can expect to hear something.
3. After the interview
   a. Be sure to make a record of your impression, review your notes, and complete any standardized form your organization may provide.
   b. Once a decision is made, you should communicate this to applicants in writing or be prepared to receive calls of inquiry.

B. Interviewee responsibilities
   1. Prepare.
      a. Look for leads.
      b. Develop a résumé. In one to two pages, provide prospective employers with your
         (1) name, address, phone number (fax number and e-mail may be included also);
         (2) career objective;
         (3) education and training;
         (4) work experience;
         (5) relevant professional licenses, awards, and honors;
         (6) hobbies and recreational activities; and
         (7) references.
      c. Target your cover letters. Cover letters should be brief and personalized.
      d. Do your homework.
      e. Rehearse.
   2. Being interviewed is divided into three parts.
      a. The opening is your chance to make a positive first impression.
      b. The body will mostly consist of you answering questions, but be prepared to ask some of your own. To be a successful applicant, you need to (1) connect with the employer; (2) support your qualifications; (3) be organized; (4) clarify ideas; (5) contribute to positive delivery; and (6) convey a positive image.
      c. In the close, thank the interviewer for the opportunity and inquire about the next steps.
   3. After the interview, write a follow-up letter which (1) thanks the employer; (2) stresses important points made in the interview; (3) offers to provide any additional information; and (4) provides any already requested information.

III. Performance-appraisal interviews
   A. Interviewer responsibilities
      1. Preparation includes (1) understanding the requirements of the job; (2) engaging in the process of goal setting; (3) scheduling regular evaluations; and (4) completing some type of standardized performance appraisal prior to the interview.
      2. Conducting the interview
         a. According to researcher Jack Gibb, certain behaviors contribute to a defensiveness whereas others contribute to a supportive climate.
            (1) Defensive behavior occurs when an individual perceives threat or anticipates threat. Communication behaviors that make people defensive include evaluations, control, strategy, neutrality, superiority, and, certainty.
            (2) Supportive behavior reduces the perception of threat. Gibb proposes six behaviors that reduce defensiveness and create a supportive climate. These are the opposites of the defensive-producing behaviors stated above. These include description, problem orientation, spontaneity, empathy, equality, and provisionalism.

b. Jeanne Barone and Jo Switzer offer several suggestions for constructive criticism. Criticism should be
　　　　(1) focused on work behaviors, not on general attitude or personality traits;
　　　　(2) specific;
　　　　(3) descriptive;
　　　　(4) stated in a way that promotes problem solving;
　　　　(5) limited to addressing between two and four areas for improvement; and
　　　　(6) appropriately timed.
　　c. Barone and Switzer also (1) suggest that employers and employees set performance goals collectively and (2) stress the importance of effective listening.
　3. Structure the interview with an opening, body, and close to the interaction.
　　a. In the opening, engage in but don't prolong typical preliminary behavior.
　　b. The body should focus first on the strengths and then the areas that need improvement. Finally, supervisors and workers should move on to setting goals.
　　c. Close the interview on a positive note only after you are sure the employee has had an opportunity to ask questions and offer suggestions.
　4. After the interview
　　a. Be sure to not leave any issues unresolved.
　　b. If something requires follow-up, do it.
　　c. Keep in mind that frequent rather than rare performance appraisals are the best follow-up.
B. Interviewee responsibilities
　1. Preparation
　　a. Know the company's expectations and criteria for evaluation.
　　b. Don't wait until the formal interview process to request feedback.
　　c. Prior to the interview, prepare your own list of topics to cover.
　2. Being interviewed
　　a. The key to being an effective interviewee is to listen, stick to the facts, and avoid getting angry or defensive.
　　b. Know your rights.
C. After the interview
　1. Determine what steps to take to achieve the agreed-upon goals.
　2. In between interviews, discuss your progress with your supervisor.
　3. If you have an objection to what has been said in your performance appraisal, you may have a chance to respond in writing. Decide which points, if any, are worth disputing.

TEACHING/LEARNING OBJECTIVES

After reading Chapter 11, students should:

- Be convinced of the long-term importance of mastering interviewing skills.

- Differentiate between information-gathering, employment-selection, and performance-appraisal interviews.

- Understand the responsibilities of both the interviewer and the interviewee in the interview process.

- Be aware of their legal rights and limitations in an interview.

- Describe behaviors that lead to an effective interview.

- Describe behaviors that could lead to an ineffective or unsuccessful interview.

- Set goals for improving their interviewing skills.

- Meet the learning objectives listed on page 267 in the text.

TROUBLESHOOTING

In a class where students could potentially range from first-year students to seniors, instructors must be prepared to cover interviewing skills from two opposite perspectives. On one hand, instructors may need to motivate those who don't see the immediate benefits from studying interviewing skills. This may be done through sharing information regarding the competition for jobs among new graduates. Practicing interviewing skills throughout their college careers may prove to be one edge they will have over equally qualified applicants in the future. A second edge, or motivation, might be to discuss the need for students to undertake internships to gain experience in their future job fields. Again, interviewing skills may be the only advantage they have over equally inexperienced candidates. In addition, keep in mind that in college towns competition for minimum-wage jobs is also fierce. On the other hand, for obvious reasons, seniors who face graduation might want to spend more time on interviewing than on other topic areas. Since time may not permit additional class discussions, encourage students to select topics on the subjects of job searches and interviewing for their individual and group speeches. In addition, seek out the career services or job placement center so that you can refer students to these helpful facilities.

INSTRUCTIONAL EXERCISES

1. Most college campuses have a career services center or job placement office. Invite a speaker from this office to your class. Ask this person to prepare a short presentation but primarily be prepared to answer students' questions. Inform your students that they will have the opportunity to conduct an informational interview with a representative from this office. As a group, and using Chapter 11 as guide, instruct students to prepare for this informational interview. Remind them that this is a cooperative effort and that their preparation or lack thereof reflects not only on them but on you, the instructor, as well. Incorporate one or two of the questions and the answers as test items.

2. The media bombards us with strategies to help us be more successful in our careers. Instruct students to review current periodicals to identify an article which addresses a concept or skill discussed in Chapter 11. Ask students to prepare a three-minute speech which includes (1) the name and date of the publication; (2) the topic discussed; (3) the advice given; and (4) how the topic relates to the material studied in class.

3. Organize students into groups of two. Deliberately assign students to work with classmates with whom they typically have little interaction. Instruct students to take turns interviewing each other. Specifically ask them to question one another on two frequently asked questions: (1) What are your strengths? and (2) What are your weaknesses?

JOURNAL WRITING

Much attention is given to interviewing well in order to land a job. However, there is little opportunity in a class that focuses on communication to discuss the types of companies that students want to work for. Scott and Brydon introduce the idea of supportive vs. defensive climates. Using this as a starting point, consider what you want from a company that you work for in the future. Draft a list of questions that you may someday want to ask a potential employer in an interview situation.

DISCUSSION TOPICS

Discuss what constitutes a professional and polished appearance for the interviewee. Using the content from Chapter 11 as a starting point, engage the class in a discussion of what they believe might be some *dos* and *dont's*. For example, how do the women feel about "big" hair, heavy makeup, short skirts, extremely high heels, perfume, jewelry, long fingernails, large handbags, seated position, and the like? How do the men feel about jewelry, long fingernails, suit styles and colors, hair length and cut, cologne, and the like?

Introduce the idea that an interview might take place over breakfast, lunch, or dinner. Engage the class in a discussion which addresses some potential concerns particular to this context. For example, what should one order in terms of the price and ease of eating (spaghetti or buffalo wings might not be great choices)? How about alcoholic drinks? What should you do if your potential new supervisor has food in his or her teeth? Does anybody really need the extra jolt from coffee in an interview situation?

TEST QUESTIONS

Multiple Choice

1. Questioning a source for information about one or more topics is characteristic of the
   *a. information-gathering interview.
   b. employment-selection interview.
   c. performance-appraisal interview.
   d. none of the above
   Page: 268

2. The interviewee is
   a. most responsible for guiding the interview.
   *b. the subject of an interview.
   c. the information gatherer.
   d. none of the above
   Page: 268

3. The information-gathering interview encompasses all of the following types of interviews EXCEPT
   a. interviews with experts.
   b. journalists interviewing witnesses.
   c. interviews by survey research firms.
   *d. none of the above
   Page: 268

4. Congress passed the Equal Employment Opportunity laws in the
   a. 1920s.
   b. 1950s.
   *c. 1960s.
   d. 1970s.
   Page: 272

5. According to bona fide occupational qualification standards, all of the following are legally acceptable as topics for interviewing questions EXCEPT
   *a. disabilities.
   b. education.
   c. work experience.
   d. skills.
   Page: 272

6. According to the Equal Employment Opportunity laws and the American Disabilities Act, questions regarding which of the following topics are acceptable?
   a. marital status
   b. age
   *c. previous unrelated work experiences
   d. religion
   Page: 272

7. According to the EEO law and the ADA, questions regarding which subjects are illegal to ask?
   a. age and marital status
   b. disabilities
   c. previous salary
   *d. both a and b
   Page: 272

8. Which type of interview question is considered the most effective?
   a. yes/no questions
   b. leading questions
   c. résumé questions
   *d. none of the above
   Page: 274

9. The evaluative-response question
   a. asks interviewees to make a judgment about a specific question topic.
   *b. is not a highly recommended question type.
   c. violates ADA guidelines.
   d. both a and b
   Page: 274

10. Which of the following types of questions should interviewers try to avoid?
    a. questions which combine two answers in one
    b. questions which require simple yes or no answers
    c. evaluative-response questions
    *d. all of the above
    Page: 274

11. According to the authors of your text, a résumé should include all of the following information EXCEPT
    a. relevant professional licenses, awards, and honors.
    b. hobbies and recreational activities.
    c. career objective.
    *d. marital status.
    Page: 277

12. Which of the following scholars taught us about defensive and supportive behaviors?
    a. Jeanne Barone
    *b. Jack Gibb
    c. Jo Switzer
    d. Charles J. Stewart
    Page: 287

13. The way to counter the defensive behavior of certainty is
    a. description.
    b. spontaneity.
    *c. provisionalism.
    d. flexibility.
    Page: 287

14. According to Jack Gibb, the behavior which counters evaluation is
    a. open-mindedness.
    *b. description.
    c. constructiveness.
    d. none of the above
    Page: 287

15. An effective performance-appraisal review is
    a. conducted in a standardized form.
    b. a tool to measure actual work performance.
    c. equally applied to all classes of employees.
    *d. all of the above
    Page: 292

True/False

16. Research indicates that interviewers typically make their decisions about applicants within the first 10 minutes of the interview. (False, p. 274)

17. Charles Stewart and William Cash recommend that interviewers begin asking questions in an "inverted funnel" style. (False, p. 274)

18. The authors of your text suggest that an interviewer begin asking questions based on the applicant's résumé to help initially relax the applicant by beginning with familiar material. (False, p. 274)

19. In an interview situation, most responsibilities fall on the shoulders of the interviewee. (False, pp. 271–272)

20. The Equal Employment Opportunity (EEO) laws were established in the 1950s to help protect job applicants from discrimination. (False, p. 272)

21. It is against the law to inquire about a job applicant's marital status even if the job description for which this person is applying indicates that extensive travel is required. (True, p. 272)

22. According to the authors of your text, hobbies and other recreational activities should never be included on a professional résumé. (False, pp. 277–278)

23. Despite whether or not you believe the interview went well, after the interview you should send a follow-up letter. (True, p. 285)

24. Barone and Switzer suggest that no more than five improvement areas be discussed in one particular performance-appraisal interview. (False, p. 289)

25. Double-barreled questions are an efficient and effective questioning method since they request two answers from one question. (False, p. 274)

Short Answer/Essay

26. List and explain the purposes of the three common types of interviews. (p. 268)

27. Compare and contrast the communication behaviors that are typical of the successful and unsuccessful interview. (p. 270)

28. As discussed in Chapter 11, compare and contrast the types of questions that interviewers should and should not ask. (p. 272)

29. Identify and discuss the six defensive behaviors and the six supportive behaviors discussed in Chapter 11. (p. 287)

30. In a performance-appraisal interview, indicate the responsibilities of both the interviewer and the interviewee. (pp. 286–290)

CHAPTER 12
THE NATURE OF SMALL GROUP COMMUNICATION

INTRODUCTION AND OUTLINE

Chapter 12 is the first of two chapters which focus exclusively on small group communication. It introduces students to different types of small groups and the advantages and disadvantages of working within groups. Specifically, the chapter covers:

I. The basics of groups
   A. Scott and Brydon define a **group** as three or more individuals who are aware of each other's presence, share a mutually interdependent purpose, engage in communication transactions with one another, and identify with the norms of the group.
      1. The more people in a group, the more difficult it is to manage the group. Five is about ideal.
      2. A group shares a purpose that requires mutual effort to achieve.
      3. Members communicate with one another face-to-face or sometimes using computers.
      4. Groups share **norms,** defined by Scott and Brydon as rules of conduct or patterns of behaviors that are considered customary.
   B. At least three types of groups can be identified by their purpose. They include
      1. formal and informal social groups;
      2. therapeutic recovery groups; and
      3. task-oriented groups.

II. Advantages and disadvantages of groups
   A. Psychologist Norman R. F. Maier asserts there are four advantages of groups.
      1. More information: Groups have a greater sum of knowledge and information than individuals working alone. A person may correct another or jog other people's memories to recall information. When a decision depends on a wide range of information, groups have an advantage.
      2. More approaches to problems: When the goal is to think of as many approaches as possible, groups usually have the edge.
      3. Greater acceptance of decisions: When decisions depend on the support of those affected for their success, the more involved people are in the deliberations, the better the odds of acceptance.
      4. Greater comprehension: People may better understand the results of a decision if they have participated in making it.
   B. Maier identified four disadvantages to working in groups.
      1. Social pressures to conform: Social pressures may force conformity to decisions, even when such conformity produces disaster, as in the case of the space shuttle *Challenger*.
      2. Premature solutions: Once a solution achieves a critical level of voiced support, better solutions introduced later have little chance of success.

3. Dominant individual: One person may emerge as the dominant leader of a group, via a strong personality or power position, even if that individual is not the best problem solver.
4. Goal conflict: Individual goals may conflict with the group's primary goal.

C. Maier identified five factors that help or hinder a group, depending on the situation. Scott and Brydon added the last two.
1. Disagreement
2. Conflicting interests
3. Risks
4. Time
5. Change
6. Shared versus individual responsibility
7. Anonymity

III. Groupthink
A. Yale professor of psychology Irving R. Janis has developed a theory to explain bad decision-making in groups.
B. **Groupthink** is a mode of thinking that occurs when people are deeply involved in a cohesive group, when desire for unanimity overrides a realistic appraisal of alternatives.
C. Systems of groupthink
1. Illusion of invulnerability: When a group thinks that it cannot fail, that is when it is most likely to fail.
2. Unquestioned belief in the group's inherent morality: The view that God is on your side can be a dangerous one.
3. Collective rationalizations: A group rationalizes mistakes and sometimes tries to blame failure on convenient scapegoats.
4. Stereotyped views of out-group members: The in-group negatively stereotypes those outside the group.
5. Direct pressure on dissenters: Naysayers are pressured to conform.
6. Self-censorship of dissenters: Those who might dissent from the majority remain silent.
7. Shared illusions of unanimity: There is a false perception that everyone agrees.
8. Emergence of mindguards: A leader's thinking is protected from dissenting and contradicting opinion.
D. To minimize groupthink, Janis offers seven suggestions.
1. Assign a devil's advocate: Have someone in the group responsible for challenging all ideas, even those that seem to be good ones.
2. Leaders should avoid revealing their preferences: Good leaders keep their preferences private until they have heard what others have to say.
3. Have independent groups work simultaneously: Have one or more groups work on the same problem.
4. Discuss group processes with trusted others and report back to the group: When permitted, sometimes it is useful to conduct a "reality check" to see if others outside the group think your group is on the right track.
5. Utilize outside experts: Whenever possible it is a good idea to allow outside experts to provide their input into the problem the group is trying to solve.
6. Consider "alternative scenarios" for rivals: Putting yourself in the other person's shoes is sometimes essential to avoiding groupthink.

7. Have a second-chance meeting: A second-chance meeting gives members an opportunity to reflect on their decision and change their minds if they wish.

IV. Marvin E. Shaw's research indicates that the likelihood of groupthink reflects three factors regarding the group's composition.

A. **Cohesiveness** is a measure of how attractive a group is to its members. It is the glue that holds a group together.

1. A highly cohesive group is one whose members are highly motivated to belong. Groups lack cohesiveness when they are imposed on members.

2. In comparison to low cohesive groups:

a. High cohesive groups have more extensive communication among group members.

b. High cohesive groups are more positive, friendly, and cooperative.

c. High cohesive groups exert higher influence on all members.

d. High cohesive groups have greater effectiveness in achieving goals.

e. High cohesive groups result in higher member satisfaction.

3. Ernest G. Bormann and Nancy C. Bormann suggest several ways to increase group cohesiveness.

a. Give the group a name with which group members can readily identify.

b. Establish group ceremonies and rituals which set the group apart from other groups.

c. Stress the importance of teamwork and cooperation.

d. Encourage individual group members to recognize each other's contributions.

e. Set goals that the group realistically can achieve.

f. Treat group members as people, not numbers.

B. **Compatibility** is the degree to which the members of a group meet each other's needs.

1. Psychologist W. C. Schutz has suggested that groups can potentially fill three basic interpersonal needs: (1) inclusion, (2) control, and (3) affection.

2. Compatibility has two benefits: (1) Compatible groups are more likely to achieve their goals; and (2) members of compatible groups are more satisfied.

C. The final element of group composition is the degree to which group members are homogeneous (similar to one another) or heterogeneous (dissimilar).

1. Marvin Shaw has identified the following effects of heterogeneity for groups:

a. Groups with diverse abilities are more effective than those with similar abilities.

b. Styles of communication are affected by the gender composition of the group.

c. Groups that include both males and females tend to be more effective than single-sex groups.

d. Mixed groups induce more conformity than groups of one gender.

e. The racial composition of a group can affect a group's feelings and behaviors.

f. Groups with different personality profiles are more effective than those that are homogeneous in this respect.

2. Generally, heterogeneous groups are more effective than homogeneous ones, depending on the exact nature of the task.

TEACHING/LEARNING OBJECTIVES

After reading Chapter 12, students should:

- Recognize the different groups to which they belong.

- Understand the advantages and disadvantages of working in groups to help them better determine situations in which it would be most beneficial to work in groups.

- Feel confident that they play a part in contributing to the success of completing small group assignments in class and their day-to-day experiences.

- Commit to engaging in behaviors that help to increase the group's cohesiveness.

- Understand groupthink and commit to engaging in behaviors that minimize its effects.

- Meet the learning objectives listed on page 297 in the text.

TROUBLESHOOTING

When providing students with practical experience with working in small groups, two potential problem areas immediately arise. First, most students inevitably have a negative group experience somewhere in their past. This colors their perceptions regarding upcoming small group assignments. Second, students' negative past experiences often stem from group assignments from other courses where classmates failed to complete their share of the group work. Typically, this negatively affected either group members' grades or their workload. With this in mind, be sure to stress the many benefits of working in groups and the fact that a corporate buzzword is "teamwork." Also, as discussed in Chapter 10, be sure to remind students that conflict arises from incompatible goals. Therefore, students should choose their group members wisely (e.g., they shouldn't join a group of students who are taking the class pass/fail or credit/no credit if their personal goal is to get an A on all class assignments).

INSTRUCTIONAL EXERCISES

1. Ask students to consider how many small groups they will be a member of today or on any given day. List the groups on the board to visually demonstrate the number and diversity of groups to which we belong. Ask students to identify each group as (1) a formal social group; (2) an informal social group; (3) a therapeutic recovery group; or (4) a task-oriented group.

2. Break students into their assigned small groups. Ask groups to create a list of norms that they would like to follow when meeting to work on small group assignments. Once all groups have created their lists, ask the class to share their norms and reasoning. Request that each student keep a copy of his or her group norms in their notes.

3. Develop a list of statements that one could easily agree or disagree with. Ask students to individually decide whether they agree or disagree. Next, instruct students to find a partner and collectively agree or disagree with each of the statements. Next, have two

pairs combine to make a group of four and instruct them to come to a consensus on whether they agree or disagree with the statements. Following this, combine groups of four, and so on, until the entire class must collectively agree or disagree with each of the statements. Use this exercise to demonstrate the influence of group size and dynamics on the decision-making process.

JOURNAL WRITING

The family is one of the most important groups to which we belong. Using Chapter 12 as a guide, reflect on the defining characteristics of a group and how they pertain to your traditional or chosen family system. For example, how does the size of your family affect the system? What are the purposes for the family unit? How do you communicate and what norms do you follow? Now reflect on your satisfaction with this particular group experience. Is your level of satisfaction related to the group's composition? Describe the group's composition in terms of cohesiveness, compatibility, and homogeneity/heterogeneity.

Most of us have had either a particularly good or particularly bad group experience in our past. Describe this experience. If the experience was negative, cite specific behaviors you will aim to avoid in your upcoming group experiences. If the experience was positive, what behaviors would you like to emulate?

DISCUSSION TOPICS

There is an old saying "Too many cooks spoil the broth." Engage the class in a discussion regarding whether or not they believe this statement to be true and why.

Nancy Reagan was a pioneer of the national "Just Say No" campaign to discourage drug use among America's teens. Critics of the program claimed that this approach was short-sighted and naive in that it failed to appreciate and address the powerful influence of peer pressure on today's youth. Do you agree with the critics or not? Why?

Many companies, such as Saturn, have implemented a managerial structure which eliminates many levels of the corporate hierarchy and puts more of the key decision-making authority directly in the hands of the factory workers. Engage the class in a discussion regarding the advantages and disadvantages of this trend.

TEST QUESTIONS

Multiple Choice

1. Which of the following satisfies all of the text authors' criteria of a group?
   a. a married couple
   b. customers waiting in a checkout line at a grocery store
   *c. a team of engineers discussing a design problem
   d. fans at a sporting event
   Page: 300

2. As the lines of communication increase,
   a. the group remains the same.
   *b. groups become more difficult to manage.
   c. opportunities for monitoring verbal and nonverbal behaviors increase.
   d. participation becomes easier.
   Page: 300

3. Which of the following is NOT a characteristic of a group?
   a. Members share a purpose that requires mutual effort to achieve.
   *b. Members communicate face-to-face, either verbally or nonverbally.
   c. Members share a set of rules of conduct or customary patterns of behavior.
   d. It is composed of three or more individuals.
   Page: 301

4. A rule of conduct or pattern of behavior that is followed by group members is
   a. groupthink.
   *b. a norm.
   c. a quality circle.
   d. interdependent behavior.
   Page: 301

5. Norms typically govern the behavior of which of the following?
   a. a family
   b. informal social groups
   c. task-oriented groups
   *d. all of the above
   Page: 301

6. La Leche League is an example of a/an:
   a. formal social group.
   b. informal social group.
   *c. self-help group.
   d. task-oriented group.
   Page: 303

7. An example of a decision-making group includes all of the following EXCEPT
   a. a jury.
   *b. Alcoholics Anonymous.
   c. a group of students completing a small group assignment.
   d. all of the above
   Page: 303

8. The basic principle behind brainstorming is to
   *a. generate as many approaches to a problem as possible by working within a group.
   b. have all the members of the group carefully scrutinize one proposed solution.
   c. allow others to participate in the problem-solving process so that they will be more accepting of the agreed-upon solution.
   d. allow others to participate in the problem-solving process so that they will better understand the rationale behind the agreed-upon solution.
   Page: 305

9. Social pressure to conform may result in
   a. valence.
   *b. rejection of a more correct minority opinion.
   c. dominance by one overbearing individual.
   d. goal conflict.
   Page: 306

10. The management decisions employed by some companies, which give employees more influence in decision-making on problems related to their job functions, are called
    *a. quality circles.
    b. collective consciousness.
    c. socialism.
    d. cooperative learning.
    Page: 307

11. The unnecessarily dangerous behavior to which groups are more susceptible than individuals is known as
    a. ineffective risk management.
    b. ineffective risk assessment.
    c. mindguarding.
    *d. the risky-shift phenomenon.
    Page: 309

12. All of the following are advantages to using groups EXCEPT which of the following?
    *a. Decisions can be reached faster since more people are working on the problem.
    b. There are more approaches to a problem, leading to more creative problem solving.
    c. There is a greater sum of knowledge and information in a group.
    d. Greater acceptance of decisions by those affected follows when people join in the decision-making process.
    Page: 310

13. The feeling of shared responsibility felt by members of a group
    a. is almost always positive because the group members support one another.
    b. leads to a high degree of compatibility.
    c. prevents healthy dialogue.
    *d. can be either positive or negative depending on the circumstances.
    Page: 310

14. Groupthink is defined as
    a. the shared responsibility people feel within a group.
    b. the emergence of a dominant individual who stifles minority opinion within the group.
    c. the pooling together of individual knowledge or information.
    *d. a process during which the group's preservation becomes more important than the quality of the group's decision.
    Page: 312

15. Which of the following is (are) symptoms of groupthink?
    a. a self-censorship of dissenters
    b. collective rationalization
    c. an illusion of invulnerability
    *d. all of the above
    Page: 312

16. Advisors who keep dissenting opinions from reaching their leader are acting as:
    a. pacifiers.
    b. nonconformists.
    *c. mindguards.
    d. bridge builders.
    Page: 314

17. A group leader who is worried that the group will make the decision they believe the leader wants to hear should
    *a. keep his or her own preference private until the decision has been made.
    b. employ mindguards.
    c. utilize outside experts.
    d. all of the above
    Page: 315

18. In the nominal group technique,
    a. a second-chance meeting is held to give group members a chance to reflect on their decision.
    *b. group members work individually in each other's presence and then discuss results.
    c. a devil's advocate is assigned.
    d. the nature of each individual group member's decision is kept private until the final group decision has been made.
    Page: 315

19. A group whose members are highly motivated to belong
    a. has more communication among group members.
    b. is highly cohesive.
    c. is more susceptible to bad decision-making when in groupthink mode.
    *d. all of the above
    Page: 316

20. The degree to which members of a group meet each other's needs is called
    a. inclusion.
    *b. compatibility.
    c. cohesiveness.
    d. homogeneity.
    Page: 318

21. Which of the following statements about diversity within a group is false?
    a. Gender-mixed groups induce more conformity than single-sex groups.
    b. Groups with diverse abilities are more effective that those with similar abilities.
    *c. Gender-mixed groups are less effective than single-sex groups.
    d. Groups with different personality profiles are more effective than those that are homogeneous.
    Page: 318

True/False

22. A social circle of students who just hang out together does NOT meet the criteria of a group because the students have no common goals. (False, p. 302)

23. According to the authors of your text, groups are a valuable form of communication which are more effective than individuals at problem-solving in all but a few highly unusual cases. (False, p. 304)

24. Disagreement within a group can be a positive force, leading to more effective group decision-making. (True, p. 309)

25. After the group has made a decision, it is a good idea to have another meeting or opportunity for group members to change their minds. (True, p. 316)

26. If a group is in a groupthink mode, a better decision may be made if the group lacks a high degree of cohesiveness. (True, p. 317)

Short Answer/Essay

27. In Chapter 12, students learn that many group behaviors can serve to both help and hinder group performance. List and explain at least five such factors. Be sure to cite specific examples. (p. 309)

28. According to Irving R. Janis, eight symptoms are characteristic of groupthink. (p. 312) List and explain these symptoms and discuss ways that groups can minimize the likelihood of entering the groupthink mode. (p. 314)

29. Imagine that you have been assigned to a task-oriented group that seems to lack cohesiveness but is charged with solving a pressing problem. What steps or strategies could you employ to increase the likelihood of the group's success? (p. 317)

30. Explain how a group's size could potentially be an advantage or a disadvantage. (p. 300)

31. Explain the similarities and differences between group cohesiveness and compatibility. (p. 316)

CHAPTER 13
SMALL GROUP COMMUNICATION IN PRACTICE

INTRODUCTION AND OUTLINE

Chapter 13 builds on the ideas introduced in Chapter 12 but focuses on group processes that lead to constructive group outcomes. Specifically, Chapter 13 discusses:

I. Group development
   A. Phases of group development include (1) orientation, (2) conflict, (3) emergence, and (4) reinforcement
      1. The orientation phase involves efforts by group members to reduce their uncertainty about one another and the task at hand.
      2. The conflict phase involves the necessary argument and disagreement involved in reaching a decision.
      3. In the emergence phase, dissent and conflict are on the decline and consensus may begin to emerge.
      4. In the reinforcement phase, groups have successfully completed their goal and seek reinforcing comments from one another.
   B. Following are steps in group problem solving.
      1. Many researchers believe groups are more productive when they follow a predetermined sequence of steps.
      2. As a result, many group discussion agendas are based on the concept of **reflective thinking,** defined as a deliberative process that requires group members to evaluate the evidence and reasoning offered as support of a claim.
      3. Researchers Wagner and Arnold apply the principles of reflective thinking to a group process using the following six steps:
         a. Define and limit the problem question.
         b. Analyze and evaluate the problem.
         c. Establish criteria or standards by which solutions will be judged acceptable or unacceptable.
         d. Examine the consequences of each available solution.
         e. Select the preferred solution or solutions.
         f. Put the preferred solution into effect.
   C. Following are principles of group problem solving regardless of the particular steps followed.
      1. Focus on understanding the problem before thinking and talking about how to solve it.
      2. Begin with a simple, unambiguous problem question.
      3. Map (explore) the problem thoroughly.
      4. Be sure that group members agree on the criteria that will guide their choices.
      5. Defer judgment when seeking solutions until you have explored the range of alternatives.

6. Use constructive arguments and other techniques to avoid groupthink.
7. Plan how to implement and follow up on solutions.

II. Roles and functions in groups
  A. A **role** is a profile of functional behaviors that a member performs for a group.
  B. The specific behavioral functions that constitute group roles fall into three classifications: (1) task, (2) relationship, and (3) self-centered.
    1. Task functions help the group accomplish its task. See pages 329–330 in *Dimensions of Communication* for a list and descriptions of task roles.
    2. Relationship functions help to maintain the group's harmony. See pages 330-331 for a list and descriptions of relationship roles.
    3. Self-centered functions can disrupt the group's process. See page 332 for a list and descriptions of self-centered roles.

III. Leadership and leaders
  A. **Leadership** is defined as influence exerted through communication that helps a group clarify and achieve goals.
  B. A **leader** is a person who exercises goal-oriented influence in a group.
  C. People can become leaders in a variety of ways including: (1) they may exercise leadership functions; (2) the group may self-identify them as leaders; or (3) they may be officially designated leaders.
  D. Leadership styles include (1) autocratic, (2) democratic, and (3) laissez-faire, which are compared in Table 13-1 on page 334 in *Dimensions of Communication*.
  E. Situational leadership is a leadership model which assumes that different leadership styles are appropriate in different situations.
    1. The variables in leadership styles rest in
      a. the amount of guidance and direction (task behavior) a leader gives;
      b. the amount of socioemotional support (relationship behavior) a leader provides; and
      c. the readiness (maturity) level that followers exhibit in performing a specific task, function, or objective.
    2. This model leads to a fourfold typology of leadership: (1) telling, (2) selling, (3) consulting, and (4) delegating.
  F. A leader has responsibilities.
    1. Demonstrate competence and character.
    2. Appear similar enough to group members that they consider you one of them, but dissimilar enough that they believe you have something to offer that they don't.
    3. Ensure that the specific functions are attended to.
      a. Determine a meeting time and place.
      b. Develop an agenda.
      c. Keep the discussion on track.
      d. Ask questions to promote discussion.
      e. Summarize and make transitions to other points.
      f. Set the agenda for the next meeting.
      g. Keep a record of meetings.
      h. See that the final group decision is accurately reported.

IV. Group member responsibilities
  A. The above leadership responsibilities can be performed by anyone in the group, not just the designated leader.

B. Following are guidelines for effective group participation.
1. Be prepared.
2. Be there.
3. Focus on ideas, not personalities.
4. Use critical thinking skills to avoid groupthink.
5. Keep your commitments to the group.

V. Presenting group decisions
A. Basic topics in a **written report** include (1) introduction; (2) statement of the problem; (3) background of the problem; (4) causes of the problem; (5) recommendations for solving the problem (including steps for implementing the solutions); and (6) appendices (for any background documents).
B. **Individual oral reports** require that a group spokesperson orally present all of the elements (as stated above) which are included in a written report.
C. A **panel discussion** is an interactive group discussion which blends preparation and spontaneity.
1. Members comment on another's points, ask questions, and openly discuss points.
2. The leader acts as a moderator who calls on members, keeps the discussion on track, and facilitates the question-and-answer period.
3. The outline of a panel discussion is similar to that of an individual report, but requires that all members comment on each topic area.
D. The **symposium** is similar in content to the panel discussion, but it lacks interactiveness and spontaneity since members prepare a mini-speech on a topic.

TEACHING/LEARNING OBJECTIVES

After reading Chapter 13, students should:

- Recognize the different phases of group development in the groups to which they belong, in and out of class.

- Recognize the advantages of engaging in reflective thinking.

- Develop a clear process for group decision making.

- Determine their individual roles and the functions that these roles serve in their small group interactions.

- Determine if the roles they hold are personally acceptable.

- Determine their individual leadership style.

- Understand the connection between leadership and group members' responsibilities.

- Feel confident that they play a part in contributing to the success of completing small group assignments in class and their day-to-day experiences.

- Meet the learning objectives listed on page 323 in the text.

INSTRUCTIONAL EXERCISES

1. Break students into their assigned groups. Ask students to reflect on Chapters 12 and 13 and the important information that they learned about small group interactions from this reading and from class discussions and exercises. Ask students to assume that they have the responsibility of teaching a group of people the basics about small group communication. In other words, they have an opportunity to tell their friends who might take this class in the future everything they need to survive your course and the small group experience. Echoing Robert Fulghum's best-selling book *All I Ever Needed to Know I Learned in Kindergarten*, ask students to create the "All I Ever Needed to Know About Small Groups I Learned in (your course call number)." Have groups share their lists.

2. Before students are assigned Chapter 13, engage the class in a task that involves group problem solving. The goal of this exercise is to demonstrate to students that they are already familiar with many of the steps to effective problem solving because this is an activity that they partake in often. You may prefer to create a scenario in which groups must come to some type of solution or action. Or you could make it a little more interesting by creating a scavenger hunt. If you didn't assign a library scavenger hunt, as suggested as an instructional exercise to complement Chapter 14, this might be another opportunity to do so. Or you could ask students to collect numerous things around campus such as a bus schedule, a department chair's signature, a list of the hours that the library is open, a schedule of speakers who will visit campus, and so on. The first team to collect all of the items wins. But more important than winning or group bonding, use this activity as an opportunity to ask students to reflect on the steps they undertook to achieve their goal. For example, did they divide and conquer, or did they first collectively work to brainstorm the locations where they could find the needed items? Apply the steps they mention to those described in Chapter 13.

JOURNAL WRITING

In Chapter 13, Scott and Brydon discuss different group roles and their functions. Consider the role that you play in the small groups to which you belong, both inside and outside the classroom. Is the role typically the same, or does it serve the same function whether it be task, relationship, or self-serving? Are you happy with the roles that you hold and the functions that they serve? Or would you like to see yourself, and have others see you, in a different role? If you are content with the roles you hold, consider what this means, if anything. Are you afraid of change? Do you feel unqualified to make a change? If you are unhappy, what steps can you take to change your image and/or your behavior?

DISCUSSION TOPICS

Discuss the following quote within the context of group effectiveness: "There is no limit to what you can accomplish if you don't care who gets the credit."

Ask students to consider how certain people come to occupy particular roles. For example, we learn in Chapter 13 that leaders may be appointed or may simply begin exercising leadership functions (p. 332). But what about other roles? Do students agree that some roles seem to be self-selected while others may be somewhat "assigned"? What should you do if you are in a role which no longer suits your needs or the needs of a group?

TEST QUESTIONS

Multiple Choice

1. The developer of the four-phase model of group development was
   a. Russell H. Wagner.
   b. Carroll C. Arnold.
   *c. B. Aubrey Fisher.
   d. John K. Brilhart.
   Page: 324

2. When members of a group are just becoming acquainted, they are in which phase of group development?
   a. forming.
   *b. orientation.
   c. acquaintance.
   d. emergence.
   Page: 324

3. The phase of group development that most likely involves a decline in group dissent and conflict is
   a. reinforcement.
   *b. emergence.
   c. orientation.
   d. conflict resolution.
   Page: 324

4. The phase of group development during which a consensus may begin to form is called
   a. reinforcement.
   b. orientation.
   *c. emergence.
   d. acquaintance.
   Page: 324

5. Reach-testing explains
   *a. the idea that groups move in a cyclical or spiral fashion through group development phases.
   b. when dissent and conflict are on the decline and a group consensus is near.
   c. a deliberative process that requires group members to evaluate the evidence and reasoning offered as support of a claim.
   d. when arguments and disagreement are encouraged in groups in order to avoid prematurely accepting a single solution.
   Page: 324

6. "A deliberative process that requires group members to evaluate the evidence and reasoning offered as support of a claim" best describes
   a. the second phase of group development, conflict.
   *b. reflective thinking.
   c. groupthink.
   d. group collaboration.
   Page: 325

7. The process of reflective thinking was defined by
   *a. John Dewey.
   b. B. Aubrey Fisher.
   c. John K. Brilhart.
   d. Kenneth H. Blanchard.
   Page: 325

8. When aiming to analyze and evaluate the problem, it is suggested you spend valuable time considering which of the following?
   a. what symptoms suggest that a problem really exists
   b. what causes produced the problem
   c. what forces are already at work to solve the difficulty
   *d. all of the above
   Page: 326

9. According to small group communication expert John K. Brilhart, the first step that groups should follow when faced with solving a problem is to
   a. develop a single, unambiguous problem question which clearly states the problem they are trying to solve and what they hope to achieve.
   *b. focus on understanding the problem before thinking and talking about how to solve it.
   c. be sure that group members agree that there is a problem and agree on criteria that will guide their choices.
   d. decide on the roles that individual group members will fulfill in the decision-making process.
   Page: 326

10. "A profile of functional behaviors that a member performs for a group" defines
    a. a task function.
    b. a norm.
    *c. a role.
    d. a social function.
    Page: 328

11. Specific behaviors that constitute group roles can be classified as all of the following EXCEPT
    a. task roles.
    b. aocial roles.
    c. self-centered roles.
    *d. functional roles.
    Page: 328

12. Which of the following is a subset of group task functions?
    a. harmonizing, dramatizing, tension-relieving
    *b. information seeking, evaluating, recording
    c. recognition seeking, withdrawing, blocking
    d. establishing norms, supporting, initiating, and orienting
    Page: 329

13. Group-maintenance functions are synonymous with
    a. task functions.
    *b. relationship functions.
    c. self-serving functions.
    d. group norms.
    Page: 330

14. Gatekeeping describes
    a. the task function of coordinating group members' input.
    b. the self-centered function of blocking information input.
    *c. the relationship function of controlling the flow of information.
    d. the task function of coordinating members' busy schedules.
    Page: 331

15. Dramatizing involves
    a. withdrawing verbally and nonverbally when upset with group members.
    b. exaggerating the possible outcomes in order to gain support for your position.
    c. using humor to relieve tensions when conflict arises.
    *d. telling stories and reliving events to build group solidarity.
    Page: 331

16. Self-centered functions include which of the following?
    *a. blocking
    b. opinion giving
    c. question asking
    d. none of the above
    Page: 332

17. A person who exercises goal-oriented influence in a group is considered
    a. a reflective thinker.
    b. a gatekeeper.
    *c. a leader.
    d. a competent communicator.
    Page: 332

18. People become leaders through
    a. self-appointing.
    b. being officially designated by others.
    c. beginning to exercise leadership functions.
    *d. all of the above
    Page: 332

19. All of the following are leadership styles identified by psychologists Lewin, Lippitt, and White EXCEPT
    a. democratic.
    *b. dictatorial.
    c. autocratic.
    d. laissez-faire.
    Page: 334

20. The U.S. Armed Forces most often function with which kind of leadership?
    a. democratic
    b. laissez-faire
    c. situational
    *d. autocratic
    Page: 334

21. People who are moderately to highly mature, able to take responsibility, but unwilling to follow a leader's direction, should be managed with which typology of leadership?
    a. telling
    b. selling
    *c. consulting
    d. delegating
    Page: 336

22. When it appears that everyone agrees on a particular issue, the leader should
    a. set the agenda for the next meeting.
    b. encourage members to tell detailed stories in support of the majority opinion.
    c. propose more discussion on the topic.
    *d. summarize the agreed-upon point and make a transition to another topic.
    Page: 339

23. One of the most frequent complaints students voice about fellow group members is
    a. refusal to go along with majority opinion.
    *b. failure to appear at scheduled meetings.
    c. personality conflicts.
    d. failure to participate in group discussions and decision-making.
    Page: 340

True/False

24. A group which fails to go through the conflict phase is likely to succumb to groupthink. (True, p. 324)

25. One of the biggest problems most groups face is the issue of proliferation, or progressing too rapidly through the orientation stage. (False, p. 325)

26. According to researchers Wagner and Arnold, the most important first step a group must take in problem solving is to establish criteria by which solutions will be judged acceptable or unacceptable. (False, p. 325)

27. One principle of group problem solving suggests that task-oriented groups defer judgment when seeking solutions. (True, p. 328)

28. Some group norms are directly transferred from society. (True, p. 330)

29. The best leaders have a predictable leadership style which remains constant in all situations. (False, p. 336)

30. The best way to get a group that has strayed from the main topic back on task is with a tactful suggestion or humorous "nudge." (True, p. 339)

31. According to the authors of your text, the symposium format of presentation is preferred because it is the most spontaneous and interesting. (False, p. 345)

Short Answer/Essay

32. Reflective thinking has been researched by the American philosopher John Dewey and scholars Russell H. Wagner and Carroll C. Arnold, among others, and applied to the small group process. Explain the concept and steps of reflective thinking as it relates to small groups. (p. 325)

33. Explain the difference between treating the symptoms and attacking the real problem. Cite specific examples to clarify your explanation. (p. 327)

34. In Chapter 13, we learn about four styles of leadership. List and explain these styles and indicate which you believe to be the most effective and why. (p. 334)

CHAPTER 14
PREPARING TO SPEAK

INTRODUCTION AND OUTLINE

A speech that lacks adequate audience analysis or clear organization is destined to be dubbed ineffective. In Chapter 14, Scott and Brydon lead students through the process of creating an effective speech step-by-step. Specifically, the chapter discusses:

I. Analyzing the situation
  A. **Audience-focused speaking** requires the speaker to consider the process of giving a speech as a transaction between the speaker and audience.
    1. Audience analysis requires the speaker to
      a. assess the accuracy of current perceptions and attributions about the people to whom he or she will be speaking;
      b. assess the cultural, group, and individual diversity of the audience; and
      c. determine if the purpose of the speech is appropriate for the audience.
    2. Audience-responsive speakers recognize that every audience is different and audience analysis is an ongoing activity.
  B. **Selecting an audience-focused purpose** requires the speaker to consider his or her general and specific purpose for giving the speech in relation to the audience.
    1. The **general purpose** is the primary function of a speech and typically aims to inform, persuade, or entertain an audience.
      a. Persuasive speeches may seek change, or they may seek to reinforce social values and/or to inoculate people against opposing viewpoints.
      b. These three general purposes are not mutually exclusive.
        (1) A persuasive speech will also inform.
        (2) An informative speech should be interesting enough that it at least persuades the audience to listen.
    2. The **specific purpose** is the goal or objective you hope to achieve in speaking to a particular audience.
  C. To **choose an audience-focused topic,** consider the following criteria.
    1. The topic should interest you.
    2. It should interest your audience or at least be capable of being made interesting.
    3. It should be appropriate for your audience.
    4. It should be appropriate to the situation.
    5. It should be appropriate for the time available.
    6. It should be manageable.
      a. Don't pick a topic beyond your abilities or limits.
      b. One of your greatest assets in speaking is your own **credibility,** or the degree to which your audience trusts and believes in you.
    7. It should be worthwhile.

II. Inventing your speech
   A. **Invention** is the creative process by which the substance of a speech is developed.
   B. There are many resources that a speaker can turn to for gathering material on a topic.
      1. Use personal experience and knowledge.
      2. Use library resources and follow these five steps:
         a. Select key terms.
         b. Search the library catalog.
         c. Search relevant indexes and abstracts.
         d. Use CD-ROM searches.
         e. Consult reference books.
      3. Conduct interviews.
      4. Use nonprint media including films, videotapes, recordings, and so on.
      5. Access Internet resources including e-mail, chat lines, usenet groups, and the World Wide Web.
   C. Keep track of your sources systematically.
      1. Construct a preliminary biography of sources you have found.
      2. Document facts and quotations to build credibility in your speech.
      3. Organize source materials in a logical manner.

III. Organizing your speech
   A. Monroe's motivated sequence is a five-step organizational scheme which includes the following five steps.
      1. Attention: Gain your audience's attention (introduction).
      2. Need: Show the audience that a need exists and affects them (body).
      3. Satisfaction: Present the solution to the need.
      4. Visualization: Help the audience imagine how their need will be met in the future (body).
      5. Action: State what action must be taken to fulfill the need (conclusion).
   B. Malandro's model organizes the speech into the traditional introduction, body, and conclusion and the following six steps.
      1. Open with impact (introduction).
      2. Focus on the thesis statement (introduction).
      3. Connect with the audience (introduction).
      4. Present the main points (body).
      5. Summarize the main points (conclusion).
      6. Close with impact (conclusion).
   C. Structuring the body of the speech effectively requires the following elements.
      1. **Main points:** The key ideas that support the thesis statement.
      2. **Subpoints:** An idea that supports a main point.
      3. A **supporting point:** An idea that supports a subpoint.
      4. **Signposts:** Transitional statements that bridge the main points of a speech.
      5. Any of the following are useful **organizational patterns.**
         a. A **time pattern** is a pattern of organization based on chronology or a sequence of events.
         b. An **extended narrative** is a pattern of organization in which the entire body of the speech is the telling of a story.
         c. A **spatial pattern** is a pattern of organization based on physical space or geography.

d. A **categorical pattern** is a pattern of organization based on natural divisions in the subject manner.

e. A **problem-solution** pattern (or stock issues approach) is a pattern of organization that analyzes a problem in terms of (1) harm, (2) significance, and (3) cause, and that proposes a solution which is: (1) described, (2) feasible, and (3) advantageous.

TEACHING/LEARNING OBJECTIVES

After reading Chapter 14, students should:

- Commit to selecting speech topics that are interesting to them and worthwhile for the audience.

- Realize the role that the audience should play in the speaker's preparation process.

- See the value of preparing a speech outline.

- Have an opportunity to be in the library.

- Begin preparation for their speech.

- Meet the learning objectives listed on page 351 in the text.

TROUBLESHOOTING

The idea of creating a formal outline to accompany a speech may seem foreign, time-consuming, and/or unnecessary to students who are taking a class which focuses on oral communication. Be prepared to discuss the importance of outlines and the functions they serve. For example, outlines provide instructors with a clear idea of what the speaker is trying to say. Furthermore, they serve as a tool that can be used to give students credit for things that the instructor failed to hear, but can clearly read. Most important, outlines provide students with an opportunity to clearly formulate their ideas prior to speaking.

INSTRUCTIONAL EXERCISES

1. Arrange for a tour of your university or college library. Ask the staff member to specifically focus on the types of sources most useful to public speakers such as indexes and abstracts, periodicals, and CD-ROM and other databases.

2. Have students partake in a library scavenger hunt with other members of their assigned small groups. You may want to have a different variation of the items to be collected for each group. Regardless, be sure to alert library staff of your assignment and the possible influx of similar questions they might receive. You might have students do the following:

    - Find the *New York Times* published on the dates of their individual births. Have them attach copies of the first page of each day.

    - Find the author, publisher, call number, and copyright date for items such as a compact disc, a video recording, a scholarly journal in communication, and/or a book. Check your library in advance and locate a specific item meeting each of the above descriptions. Students then need to find the information on *The Book of Quotes* or whatever item you choose, write it down, and bring it in.

- If available in your library, find *Great Speeches from the 20th Century* in nonprint media. Have students list one speech from each volume. If you have time, instruct them to listen to and/or evaluate one.

- Using the main catalog system, ask students to find out how many references on the subject of relaxation are housed in the library. Instruct them to find and attach a copy of a relaxation technique that might help control speech anxiety. Note this technique does not have to state that it is explicitly for curbing speech anxiety. Many techniques could be adapted for this purpose.

- Ask students to provide the specific location of the following in your library:
  - bound periodicals
  - current periodicals
  - microfilm readers
  - reference materials
  - the on-line catalog
  - CD-ROM and other databases
  - *Reader's Guide to Periodical Literature*

3. Copy the following outline and cut it apart into sections that are not labeled. Paste content sections and the parts of an organized speech (in bold) on three-by-five-inch index cards. Students must organize the speech working in small groups. Floor or table space will be needed so that students can move pieces around until they logically fit together. The following outline is formatted so that you can simply copy, cut, and paste.

Introduction

Open with impact: Students—you can afford international travel.

Focus: It is possible to travel cheaply if you learn to manage your money.

Connect with audience: As college students, we have a desire to travel to the places we have learned about, but because of our student status you might think you don't have the funds to do so. A trip to Europe or anywhere else doesn't have to cost thousands of dollars if you learn to save here and there, and to budget.

Body

Preview: Today, I'm going to share with you how to save money while preparing the essentials for your trip abroad. Then, I will show you how to see the sights and travel on a budget once you get to your destination. And finally, I will share some tips with you that will help you stick to your inexpensive itinerary.

I. Main Point:

Before you leave on your dream vacation, there are many preparations you must make in advance.

Subpoint A:

First, you must decide on where you would like to visit.

Supporting point one:

You might want to look at the exchange rates and decide where you could get the most for the American dollar.

    a. These figures are provided in daily papers in the business section.
    b. Realize that if you travel at a time or to a place where the value of the dollar is down, you will spend a lot more money.

Supporting point two:

Determine if you will need a visa, passport, both a visa and a passport, or if an original copy of your birth certificate will be enough.

    a. A passport costs $50 and takes about eight weeks to obtain.
    b. Arrangements for a visa must be made through the government well in advance.
    c. An original birth certificate will probably be found in your parents' records, but if not call the city of your birth.

        1. Using a birth certificate will save money, but it is not accepted everywhere.
        2. It must be the original with the raised seal to be accepted anywhere.
        3. I suggest you bring backup identification as well.

Subpoint B:

Next, you must decide how to best get there.

Supporting point one:

In some cases, you may travel by boat, but most often students travel by plane.

Supporting point two:

If you will be traveling by plane, buy your airline ticket 6–9 months in advance to save.

    a. Call discount travel services.
    b. Check with airline ticket consolidators.
    c. Watch the travel section in your local newspaper.

Signpost: Now that you are ready to leave the United States, you must decide on a method of travel.

II. Main Point:

There are two primary methods of travel available to students.

Subpoint A:

A variety of companies offer guided tours which take care of all of your arrangements, but these tend to be very expensive.

Subpoint B:

By planning your own lodging, backpacking, and reading budget guide books to help you plan your itinerary, you can save a fortune.

Supporting point one:

Students can purchase discount cards from a local travel agency.

   a. An International Student Identity Card costs approximately $20 and entitles students to discounts at numerous participating hotels and attractions.
   b. An International Youth Hostel Association card costs approximately $25 and entitles bearers to stay at youth hostels worldwide for approximately $10–$20 per night.

Supporting point two:

You will need a backpack, raincoat, a good pair of walking shoes, and possibly a sleeping bag and a bike.

   a. I suggest you spend the extra cash to get a good pair of walking shoes, but plan well enough in advance to catch a sale.
   b. By bringing a bike, you can save money on inter-city transportation.
   c. Another inexpensive method of travel is the Eurorail.

      1. Eurorail tickets can be purchased for varied lengths of stay and choice destinations.
      2. Eurorails can be purchased through a local travel agent or by calling Europass at 1-800-848-7245.

Supporting point three:

To help you determine the sights you would like to see, purchase *Let's Go: The Budget Guide to Europe* or another discount guide book.

Signpost: Now that you have undergone the necessary preparation that allows you to save valuable dollars, we need to talk about how to stay on your budget while traveling.

III.   **Main Point**:

Staying on a budget is the biggest challenge students face while traveling abroad.

Subpoint A:

Use a budget guide book to determine which sights you would like to visit and their cost before arriving at your destination.

Subpoint B:

Avoid eating at locations that are primarily tourist traps.

Supporting point one:

Be aware that most European restaurants charge to sit down and for bread and water.

Supporting point two:

With this in mind, food to go and a park bench are often your best chance at saving money.

Subpoint C:

Shop around for the best exchange rates. Often using a credit card is your best option since then you are guaranteed bank exchange rates versus the lower rates that are typically offered to tourists.

Subpoint D:

Avoid the temptation to buy souvenirs. Bring your camera and lots of film, and your pictures and memories will be the best souvenirs of all.

Conclusion

I. **Summarize:**   Traveling to Europe is a priceless opportunity for students, but as you learned today, it doesn't have to leave you penniless. You can (1) prepare well in advance; (2) make all of your plans yourself; (3) take advantage of discount opportunities available to students; and (4) follow practical steps to help you stay on your budget.

II. **Close with impact:**   Now go, make plans to create memories that will last a lifetime. Just remember, follow the steps discussed here today so that the bills won't last a lifetime too.

JOURNAL WRITING

Chapter 14 explains the value of focusing on the audience when preparing a speech. In what ways, if any, is undergoing the process of audience analysis useful in your one-on-one interactions? How often do you consider the other person in your communication trans-action? How often *should* you consider the other person in your communication transactions? In what ways could adequate audience analysis help your personal as well as professional relationships?

DISCUSSION TOPICS

Engage the class in a discussion of effective ways to open and close a speech with impact. Make a list on the board and encourage students to keep this list in their notes.

Ask the class to suppose that they are listening to a speech and detect that the speaker has made a factual error in the material that he or she has presented. Engage the class in a discussion as to what they should do. Are there any variables that they should consider, such as the degree to which this incorrect piece of information relates to the rest of his or her argument? Does it depend on who the speaker is? Refer to Chapter 5 on ethical communication. Remind students of their ethical responsibilities, but discuss the difficulties of sometimes living up to them.

TEST QUESTIONS

Multiple Choice

1. What do Dwight D. Eisenhower, William Safire, Arthur Schlesinger, Jr., and Peggy Noonan have in common?
   a. They all experienced high speech anxiety.
   *b. They all wrote speeches for famous people.
   c. They are all role models for effective public speaking.
   d. all of the above
   Page: 351

2. When speakers begin to focus on the needs of the audience, they are engaging in the process of
   a. reflective thinking.
   *b. audience analysis.
   c. Malandro's motivational sequence.
   d. aiversity-responsive communication.
   Page: 352

3. The audience in a public speaking situation is best understood as
   a. the individuals who share and listen to a public speech.
   b. a necessary part of the communication transaction.
   c. a diverse group that speakers must assess prior to giving a speech.
   *d. all of the above
   Page: 353

4. When engaging in audience analysis, the speaker must consider which levels of audience diversity?
   a. whether they need to be persuaded, informed, or entertained
   *b. cultural, group, and individual
   c. both a and b
   d. neither a nor b
   Page: 353

5. Audience-focused speaking involves
   a. considering group diversity.
   b. considering the purpose of the speech.
   *c. both a and b
   d. neither a nor b
   Page: 353

6. Audience analysis is
   a. an activity that takes place only before giving a speech.
   *b. an activity that should take place before and after giving a speech.
   c. a static activity.
   d. an activity that requires great skill and therefore is accomplished only by the most skilled speakers.
   Page: 353

7. A specific purpose of a speech is
   a. to inform an audience.
   b. to persuade an audience.
   c. both a and b
   *d. neither a nor b
   Page: 354

8. The speaker's goal or objective in speaking to a particular audience is called the
   a. focus statement.
   b. thesis statement.
   *c. specific purpose.
   d. general purpose.
   Page: 354

9. A speaker's specific purpose should
   a. describe the results he or she seeks.
   b. express his or her goals in measurable terms.
   c. set a realistic goal.
   *d. all of the above
   Page: 354

10. A speech which aims to reinforce existing social values is best described as
    a. an informative speech.
    b. a speech of inoculation.
    *c. a persuasive speech.
    d. none of the above
    Page: 354

11. When you are selecting your speech topic, the authors of your text suggest all of the following EXCEPT
    a. selecting a topic that is interesting to you.
    b. selecting a topic that can be made interesting to your audience.
    *c. considering which organizational model you are most comfortable with employing.
    d. considering whether the topic is manageable.
    Page: 354

12. To persuade, to inform and to entertain are all examples of
    a. specific purposes.
    b. speech purposes.
    *c. general purposes.
    d. all of the above
    Page: 354

13. When the authors of your text suggest that students select a topic that is manageable, they are specifically referring to
    a. avoiding topics that are beyond your abilities and resources.
    b. avoiding topics that will undermine your credibility with the audience.
    c. avoiding topics that your audience knows more about than you do.
    *d. all of the above
    Page: 355

14. The process by which the substance of the speech is developed is known as
    a. brainstorming.
    b. sequencing.
    *c. invention.
    d. previewing.
    Page: 356

15. Monroe's motivated sequence includes which set of steps?
    a. opening with impact; establishing need; connecting this need to the audience; proposing solutions; calling for action
    *b. getting your audience's attention; demonstrating a need that affects them; presenting a solution; helping the audience visualize how this solution will help meet the established need; stating what actions must be taken to fulfill the need
    c. opening with impact; focusing your audience's attention on the thesis of your speech which revolves around an audience need; connecting this need to your audience; presenting solutions that fulfill this need; helping the audience to visualize the satisfaction they will receive from implementing the presented solutions; suggesting steps for action
    d. none of the above
    Page: 365

16. Monroe's motivated sequence is best suited to
    a. organizing an informative speech.
    *b. organizing a persuasive speech.
    c. Both a and b are equally suited.
    d. neither a nor b
    Page: 366

17. Most speeches are organized into these main parts:
    *a. introduction, body, conclusion
    b. attention, need, solution
    c. main points, subpoints, supporting points
    d. It depends on which model or organization you are following.
    Page: 366

18. According to Malandro's model of organization, you should
    a. organize material in chronological order.
    b. organize your speech based on the natural divisions of the subject matter.
    c. organize the entire body of the speech as if telling a story.
    *d. none of the above
    Page: 366

19. According to Malandro's model, all of the following should be included in the introduction EXCEPT
    a. an attention-grabbing opening statement.
    *b. a brief overview of the main points to be presented in the body.
    c. a clear thesis statement.
    d. none of the above
    Page: 366

20. A thesis statement
    a. informs your audience of your general purpose.
    *b. expresses the central point of your speech.
    c. opens with impact.
    d. none of the above
    Page: 367

21. After opening and focusing, what is the next step in your speech?
    *a. connecting with your audience
    b. previewing your main points
    c. transitioning into your first main point
    d. summarizing your first main point
    Page: 367

22. Which of the following help to effectively structure a speech?
    a. main points and subpoints
    b. signposts
    c. organizational patterns
    *d. all of the above
    Page: 368

23. In an outline, the A, B, and C points are called
    a. main points.
    *b. subpoints.
    c. supporting points.
    d. It depends on how the outline is organized.
    Page: 375

24. Signposts serve the purpose of
    *a. transitioning between main points of a speech.
    b. informing the audience of the organizational pattern employed.
    c. both a and b
    d. neither a nor b
    Page: 376

25. A speech which informs the audience about key locations on the university campus would be best organized following
    a. a chronological pattern.
    b. a categorical pattern.
    *c. a spatial pattern.
    d. an extended narrative.
    Page: 378

26. A pattern based on the natural divisions of the subject matter is called
    a. causal.
    *b. categorical.
    c. spatial.
    d. time.
    Page: 379

True/False

27. To entertain an audience should not be the primary function of a speech but may more appropriately serve as a speaker's specific purpose. (False, p. 354)

28. A speech to inoculate aims to provide audience members with new information regarding a topic they may already be somewhat familiar with. (False, p. 354)

29. All effective informative speeches include persuasive appeals as well. (True, p. 354)

30. Millions of people access the Internet daily, yet the authors of your text suggest avoiding this medium for acquiring supporting material for speeches because there is no way to determine the credibility of the original source. (False, p. 362)

31. Signposts serve the function of introducing subpoints or supporting points in a speech. (False, p. 376)

Short Answer/Essay

32. List and explain the six steps of Malandro's model of organization. (p. 366)

33. Explain the statement "All informative speeches are persuasive and all persuasive speeches are informative." (p. 354)

34. Assume that you have just received your first speech assignment. According to the authors of your text, what seven criteria should you use for selecting a speech topic? (p. 354)

35. Define *credibility*. How can a speaker establish or maintain his or her credibility with an audience? (p. 355)

36. The authors of your text encourage you to consider audience diversity when preparing a speech. Explain how the three levels of diversity might influence you in this process. Be specific. (p. 353)

CHAPTER 15
PRESENTING YOUR SPEECH

INTRODUCTION AND OUTLINE

Confidence is essential for students effectively presenting speeches. In Chapter 15, Scott and Brydon explain common sources for speech anxiety and provide practical steps to help students deal with their fears. In addition, they discuss the advantages and disadvantages of the different speaking styles and the role that nonverbal communication plays in an effective presentation. Specifically, Chapter 15 covers:

I. The audience's reaction to a speech depends on the content and the **delivery,** which is defined as the nonverbal behaviors by which a speaker conveys his or her message to an audience.

II. Speech anxiety
  A. **Speech anxiety** refers to the fear of speaking in public, usually accompanied by mental worry and physical signs of excessive arousal such as perspiring, rapid heartbeat, and dry mouth.
    1. ABC's "20/20" reported that speech anxiety is regularly experienced by upwards of 40 percent of all American adults.
    2. Speech anxiety can be mental and/or physical and can happen before, during, and after a speech.
    3. Some degree of anxiety while speaking is not only normal, but also performance enhancing.
  B. Sources of speech anxiety vary among individuals. They include:
    1. Pessimistic attitudes during speaking
    2. Inadequate preparation and practice
    3. Negative or insufficient experience
    4. Unrealistic goals
    5. Inaccurate perception of the audience
    6. Negative self-talk
      a. **Self-talk** is silent communication with oneself, sometimes referred to as intrapersonal communication.
      b. **Negative self-talk** is self-criticizing, self-pressuring, and catastrophizing statements made to oneself which emphasize doubts about speaking publicly.
  C. Controlling speech anxiety involves following a series of steps that are the same for everyone regardless of your level of speech anxiety.
    1. Develop an optimistic attitude toward speaking.
    2. Don't put off preparing your speech.
    3. Look for opportunities to gain speaking experience.
    4. Set realistic goals.
    5. Realize the audience wants you to succeed.
    6. Practice **constructive self-talk,** defined as positive coping statements we make to ourselves that accentuate our assets, encourage relaxation, and emphasize realistic goals before, during, and after a speech.

7. Use visual imagery to enhance performance.
8. Use relaxation techniques.
   a. You can help your body relax if you engage in some form of intense physical exercise one to two hours before you speak.
   b. Relaxation imagery involves visualizing pleasant and calming situations.
   c. Muscular relaxation is a technique using systematic tensing and relaxing of various muscle groups.

III. Audience-focused delivery
   A. Choose an appropriate method of delivery that depends on the specific situation you face and the kind of delivery your audience is likely to expect.
      1. **Manuscript** delivery involves writing out a speech and reading it to your audience.
         a. This method may be best when the audience requires precise information or the speaker expects to be quoted.
         b. Manuscript speaking hinders the speaker's delivery because it
            (1) impedes the speaker from responding to the audience's feedback;
            (2) limits the ability to move, gesture, and make eye contact; and
            (3) demands a lectern, which is a barrier between speaker and audience.
      2. **Memorized** delivery requires committing an entire speech to memory.
         a. This method allows the speaker to concentrate on eye contact, movement, and gestures.
         b. Drawbacks include the fact that most audience members don't expect to hear a memorized speech, you could lose your mental place, and memorizing requires a lot of time.
      3. **Impromptu** delivery is a spontaneous, unrehearsed method of presenting a speech.
      4. **Extemporaneous** delivery combines careful preparation with spontaneous speaking.
         a. The speaker generally uses brief notes.
         b. This method allows you to maintain eye contact, move, gesture, and adapt to feedback.

IV. Nonverbal delivery
   A. Recall from Chapter 4 that nonverbal communication is a wordless system of communicating that is spontaneous, continuous, and uses multiple channels simultaneously.
   B. The following components of nonverbal communication are interrelated, meaning a change in one of them can produce changes in others and profoundly affect the delivery of a speech.
      1. The **environment** is the physical surrounding for a speech and the physical distance separating a speaker from the audience.
         a. Environmental characteristics such as lighting, temperature, comfort, and aesthetics will influence the speaker and the audience physically and psychologically.
         b. The layout of the room affects (1) the **zone of interaction,** which is the area in which the speaker can easily make eye contact with the audience; and (2) the amount of space physically separating the speaker from the audience.

2. As discussed in Chapter 4, the significance of **appearance** to public speaking can be measured in at least two ways.
    a. Audience members use appearance to initially judge a speaker's level of credibility and attractiveness.
    b. How the speaker perceives him- or herself as a result of appearance will impact the speaker's self-confidence.
    c. At minimum speakers should control their dress. Clothes should be appropriate to the situation.
3. The **face and eyes** are useful in communicating friendliness to an audience, reducing an undesirable feeling of distance, and promoting immediacy.
    a. The best speakers don't simply make eye contact with the audience but with individual members of the audience as well.
    b. Keep in mind that norms for appropriate eye contact are culturally determined, not universal.
4. To gain maximum control of your **voice,** you need to know two things: (1) the mechanics of the voice; and (2) the importance of finding your own voice rather than trying to imitate the voice of someone else.
    a. Mechanical characteristics of the voice include volume, pitch, range, rhythm, tempo, and articulation.
    b. If you are not satisfied with the sound of your own voice, work on finding your own voice by taking a voice and articulation class at your university or practicing with a tape recorder.
5. Your **gestures and movements** as you grow as a public speaker should be a refined reflection of what you do naturally.
    a. Even though gestures and movement should reflect what you do naturally, they can be purposefully used to complement your delivery in several ways.
    b. You can use gestures and movements to make your delivery more emblematic, to make it more illustrative, and to regulate the speech transaction.
        (1) An **emblem** is a meaningful and intentional gesture or movement, or a series of them, that can be translated into words.
        (2) **Illustrators** are nonverbal gestures whose purpose is to "show" what is being talked about.
        (3) **Regulators** are nonverbal gestures whose purpose is to influence the amount and type of feedback received from the audience.
    c. People make all kinds of attributions about speakers based on their **posture.**
6. **Touch** affects your delivery in two ways.
    a. **Self-adapting behaviors** are distracting touching behaviors that speakers engage in unconsciously (e.g., touching face, hair, or clothes).
    b. In instances where someone else becomes involved in your presentation, it is sometimes appropriate to touch someone in the form of shaking hands or patting someone on the back. However, exercise caution and avoid touching that can be interpreted as inappropriate.
7. **Time** potentially affects delivery in a number of ways.
    a. If you attempt to cover too much material, time may force you to hurry.
    b. The audience's perceptions of your delivery will be influenced by your timing, a term frequently used in reference to actors and comics.

c. The speed or slowness of your delivery should be coordinated with the norms of your audience.

d. Whether you are on time or late affects your credibility in this culture.

V. The functions of nonverbal communication behaviors in delivery

A. **Complementing the message** with a nonverbal cue serves to reinforce what you verbally share with your audience.

B. **Contradicting your message** nonverbally while communicating interpersonally is something speakers should try to avoid.

C. **Repeating a message** nonverbally is a way to reinforce a message by making it redundant.

D. Nonverbal messages may **substitute for a verbal cue** as in the case where a speaker raises his or her hands in an attempt to stop an audience's applause.

E. Nonverbal communication may **increase the perception of immediacy,** or psychological closeness and approachability, between the speaker and audience.

F. Convey the speaker's level of enthusiasm in an attempt to **excite the audience.**

G. **Convey power** through manipulating posture, eyes and voice, gestures and movements.

H. Understanding the functions of nonverbal behaviors enables speakers to **take a proactive approach** and engage in **proactive delivery,** defined as delivery in which a speaker takes the initiative and anticipates and controls as many variables as possible, rather than merely reacting to them.

TEACHING/LEARNING OBJECTIVES

After reading Chapter 15, students should:

- Understand that speech anxiety is normal.

- Be convinced that a certain degree of speech anxiety is performance enhancing.

- Identify their personal reasons for experiencing speech anxiety.

- Recognize the role that self-talk plays in communication anxiety.

- Commit to engaging in behaviors that help to eliminate speech anxiety.

- Practice extemporaneous speaking.

- Meet the learning objectives listed on page 385 in the text.

TROUBLESHOOTING

In a class covering public speaking, speech anxiety is a potential trouble spot on any given day of class. Therefore, it is highly recommended that you discuss the topic as early as possible in the semester or quarter. In most cases, after teaching students about the prevalence of speech anxiety, its sources, and steps to control it, most students feel more confident. However, in some instances the subject is discussed too extensively, and as a result students who experienced little speech anxiety now experience more. Or students feel that claiming speech anxiety can be the "catch all" excuse for failing to deliver an effective presentation. When discussing speech anxiety, you must communicate to your students your empathy at the same time that you avoid being so empathetic that they fail to rise to the challenge.

INSTRUCTIONAL EXERCISES

1. Break students into teams of two. Ask students to imagine the morning of their next speech assignment. Have students take turns engaging in negative and constructive self-talk respectively. As one student voices aloud a negative self-talk message, the partner is to respond with a constructive self-talk message. For example:

Partner one: This assignment really stinks.

Partner two: Public speaking skills will help me get a good job. This is a great opportunity to practice.

Each student should have a turn at stating both negative and constructive messages.

2. Most students experience difficulty maintaining eye contact with their audience members as a whole and can't imagine the day that they will be able to look into individual members' eyes while delivering a speech. Improved eye contact results from familiarity with the material and practice. Have students break into their assigned small groups. Each student is to write a 2–3-minute impromptu speech about a topic that they are extremely comfortable talking about in everyday encounters. They should aim to open and close with impact and follow basic organizational guidelines; however, the focus should not be on the content, but instead on the delivery. Each student is to deliver his or her speech to the group members. While delivering this speech, the speaker, at some point, must look into every group members' eyes. If, at the end of the speech, any group member cannot say in good conscience that the speaker made direct eye contact with him or her, the speaker must give his or her speech again, and again, and again until direct eye contact has been made with all group members.

JOURNAL WRITING

By this point, you understand that speakers never have a second chance to make a first impression. We recognize many of the common mistakes that speakers make and know which behaviors to try to avoid. At this time, consider the type of impression you would like to make. What image do you want the audience to hold of you? List some strategies for helping you to reach this end.

DISCUSSION TOPICS

Many students fear public speaking because of a prior bad experience. This is a good opportunity to have students talk about their prior speaking experiences and what they liked and didn't like about them. If you have your own experiences to share, this would be a good time to do so.

Say the words "I love you" in three ways—sincerely, sarcastically, and lustfully. This usually gets the class interested in a discussion on using their voice to convey meaning.

What makes a good public speech? Have students write down five characteristics of a poor speech they recall and five characteristics of a good speech they remember. Then have students call out as many characteristics of a good speech as they can and write these on the board. Then do the same with the characteristics of a poor speech. Discuss how students' criteria relate to those discussed in *Dimensions of Communication*. For example, did they mention disorganized speeches or speakers who are not interested in their own topic?

Discuss the advantages and disadvantages of each type of delivery style. Have students cite specific examples of each type from the media or their personal experiences. Examples include: the State of the Union Address, a toast at a wedding, the Academy Awards, commencement addresses, or even answering a question in a large lecture class.

TEST QUESTIONS

Multiple Choice

1. Speech anxiety is characterized by which of the following?
    a. experienced only before a speech
    b. the psychological dimension of performance anxiety
    c. always performance enhancing
    *d. none of the above
    Page: 386

2. Which is a common and easily prevented source of speech anxiety for students?
    a. irrational goals
    b. negative self-talk
    *c. inadequate preparation
    d. lack of physical exercise
    Page: 388

3. Self-talk that blows out of proportion the consequences of poor performance is called
    a. self-criticizing.
    b. self-pressuring.
    *c. catastrophizing.
    d. self-evaluation.
    Page: 390

4. Verbally abusing yourself about your performance is called
    *a. self-criticizing.
    b. self-pressuring.
    c. catastrophizing.
    d. self-evaluation.
    Page: 390

5. Jim is really excited about an upcoming court case. He is nervous but keeps thinking about what a great opportunity trying such a high-profile case is for career advancement. Jim is engaging in
    a. feflective thinking.
    b. self-adapting behavior.
    *c. constructive self-talk.
    d. audience-focused coping.
    Page: 391

6. Which mental technique is commonly used by athletes to control performance anxiety?
   a. systematic desensitization
   b. self-adapting behaviors
   *c. visual imagery
   d. visual relaxation
   Page: 391

7. Which technique is designed to decondition the physical tension you may feel when thinking about public speaking?
   a. constructive self-talk
   b. visual imagery
   *c. muscular relaxation
   d. self-adapting
   Page: 394

8. Positive advantages of delivering a speech using a manuscript include that
   a. speakers can concentrate on gestures and movements.
   b. speakers require a lectern, which conveys a message of power to the audience.
   c. both a and b
   *d. neither a nor b
   Page: 395

9. _____ is the most appropriate method of delivery for the State of the Union address.
   a. Extemporaneous
   b. Memorized
   *c. Manuscript
   d. Impromptu
   Page: 395

10. _____ is a spontaneous, unrehearsed method of presenting a speech.
    *a. Impromptu
    b. Extemporaneous
    c. Manuscript
    d. Memorized
    Page: 396

11. A method of speech delivery that combines careful preparation with spontaneous speaking is called
    a. impromptu.
    b. manuscript.
    *c. extemporaneous.
    d. memorized.
    Page: 396

12. Which of the following styles of presentation does the text recommend for students to use in class?
    a. manuscript
    *b. extemporaneous
    c. memorized
    d. It depends on the subject of the speech.
    Page: 396

13. Nonverbal immediacy is established through which of the following?
    a. the zone of interaction
    b. the face and eyes
    c. touch
    *d. all of the above
    Page: 397

14. According to the authors of your text, the environment is a nonverbal element of delivery which includes all of the following EXCEPT
    *a. the mood of the audience.
    b. the temperature of the room.
    c. the zone of interaction.
    d. none of the above
    Page: 398

15. The zone of interaction refers to
    a. the physical distance that separates the speaker from the audience.
    *b. the area in which a speaker can easily make eye contact with audience members.
    c. the way that the seating is arranged.
    d. all of the above
    Page: 399

16. A facet of appearance that everyone should aim to control is
    a. the face and eyes.
    *b. dress.
    c. eye contact.
    d. self-adapting behaviors.
    Page: 400

17. To use your voice effectively, it is important to control which of the following?
    a. volume
    b. pitch
    c. tempo
    *d. all of the above
    Page: 401

18. Nonverbal gestures whose purpose is to "show" what is being talked about are referred to as
    a. emblems.
    *b. illustrators.
    c. regulators.
    d. icons.
    Page: 401

19. _____ is defined as "a meaningful and intentional gesture or movement, or a series of them, that can be translated into words."
    *a. An emblem
    b. An illustrator
    c. A regulator
    d. An icon
    Page: 404

20. Based on one's posture alone, audience members are likely to make attributions about
    a. the confidence level of a speaker.
    b. how seriously the speaker regards his or her topic.
    *c. both a and b
    d. neither a nor b
    Page: 408

21. Self-adapting behaviors are
    *a. distracting to the audience.
    b. a strategy for overcoming speech anxiety.
    c. an internal mechanism for alleviating the psychological effects of speech anxiety.
    d. none of the above
    Page: 408

22. Nonverbal communication behaviors serve which of the following functions?
    a. complementing a verbal message
    b. contradicting a verbal message
    c. exciting the audience
    *d. all of the above
    Page: 409

23. Maintaining eye contact and removing physical barriers help convey
    a. power.
    *b. immediacy.
    c. friendliness.
    d. a perception of an enlarged zone of interaction.
    Page: 411

True/False

24. According to the authors of your text, delivery is the nonverbal behaviors by which a speaker conveys his or her message to an audience. (True, p. 385)

25. Performance anxiety refers to the psychological symptoms associated with giving a speech; the physical symptoms which sometimes accompany giving a presentation are known as speech anxiety. (False, p. 387)

26. According to a "20/20" report, approximately 90% of all American adults suffer from speech anxiety. (False, p. 387)

27. Some speech anxiety is not only common but desirable for an effective performance. (True, p. 388)

28. Inadequate preparation and practice is a common source of speech anxiety. (True, p. 388)

29. Self-talk can be both self-pressuring and positively reinforcing. (True, p. 390)

30. When a speaker lacks public speaking experience, a manuscript style of delivery is recommended. (False, p. 396)

31. Touching someone is sometimes appropriate in a public speech despite the rise of sexual harassment lawsuits in the United States. (True, p. 408)

32. One function of nonverbal communication is contradicting a message that is presented verbally. (True, p. 410)

33. A proactive delivery style involves the speaker appropriately reacting to unexpected circumstances in public speaking situations. (False, p. 413)

Short Answer/Essay

34. Describe the relationship between self-talk, anxiety, and performance. (pp. 391–394)

35. Explain at least five ways to control speech anxiety as discussed by the authors in Chapter 15. (p. 390)

36. Explain the differences between proactive and reactive delivery styles. Cite specific examples. (p. 413)

37. Explain the importance of appearance in delivering an effective presentation. (p. 400)

38. Define and explain emblems, illustrators, and regulators. Cite specific examples. (p. 404)

CHAPTER 16
INFORMATIVE SPEAKING

INTRODUCTION AND OUTLINE

Chapter 16 provides students with a basic theoretical understanding of the learning process and practical suggestions for creating an effective informative speech. Specifically, the chapter discusses:

I. Chapter 16 opens with a story that explains the concept of *ganas*, or the desire to succeed.
   A. *Ganas* is related to informative speaking in that an effective informative speech inspires the audience to put the information to constructive use.
   B. Informative speaking is the process by which an audience gains new information.

II. Focusing on your audience's learning styles
   A. Informative speaking and styles of learning
      1. When creating an informative speech, one important consideration is recognizing that not everyone has the same learning style.
      2. Simply, some learn by hearing, others by seeing or doing. A list of diverse learning styles appears on page 420.
      3. Good public speakers recognize these differences and appeal to as many styles as possible.
   B. The components of learning
      1. **Learning** is the acquisition of new information. Learning has three components.
         a. **Cognition** is the purely mental component of learning.
         b. **Affect** is the emotional/attitudinal component of learning.
         c. **Behavior** is the skill component of learning—the ability to do something with the knowledge acquired.
      2. Learning requires all three components.
   C. The informative-persuasive continuum
      1. Some people argue that a speech can be exclusively informative, with no purpose other than passing information along. Others argue that the distinction between an informative speech and a persuasive speech is blurred.
      2. Scott and Brydon believe that an informative speech is worthless unless it is designed to stay with the audience and influence their life in some way.
      3. The relationship between informative and persuasive speeches is one of a continuum not a dichotomy.
         a. On one end of the continuum is knowledge and on the other is behavior.
         b. Although a single speech may be predominately directed toward the informative end on the continuum, it may also contribute to the process of persuading at least some audience members to change at some point.

III. Attributes of effective informative speaking
  A. Research suggests that the likelihood of an audience perceiving information as relevant depends significantly on six message attributes.
  B. These attributes represent the criteria people use to decide whether a speaker's information is worth the time and effort to pay attention and actively process it.
    1. **Novelty:** The quality of being new and stimulating
    2. **Compatibility:** The perception that a message is consistent with attitudes, beliefs, values, and lifestyle
    3. **Comprehensibility:** The perception that a message is not too difficult or complex to understand
    4. **Relative advantage:** The perception that a message is beneficial
    5. **Observability:** The degree to which the information can be seen
    6. **Trialability:** The opportunity to experiment with an idea, a product, or a practice without penalty

IV. Modes of informative speaking
  A. There are four basic ways to inform an audience:
    1. Speeches that explain
    2. Speeches that instruct
    3. Speeches that demonstrate
    4. Speeches that describe
  B. Informative speeches may employ more than one of the above modes and should include as many of the six attributes of informative effective speaking as possible.
    1. One attribute that you need to include in every speech is compatibility.
    2. If your audience sees the topic as incompatible with their needs, beliefs, attitudes, or values, they will view your speech as a hostile persuasive attempt rather than an informative speech.

V. Strengthening your speech with presentational aids
  A. **Presentational aids** are visual, audio, and audiovisual devices that augment a speech.
  B. **Visual aids** are presentational aids that convey their message visually.
    1. Types of visual aids include (a) objects, (b) models, (c) photographs, (d) diagrams and illustrations, and (e) charts, graphs, and maps.
    2. Visual aids can be constructed from a variety of materials including (a) poster board, (b) flip charts, (c) overhead transparencies, (d) slides, (e) handouts, and (f) chalkboards.
    3. Guidelines for constructing visual aids, on page 442, revolve around (a) simplicity, (b) visibility, (c) layout, and (d) color.
  C. **Audio aids** are presentational aids that use sound only, such as recordings.
  D. **Audiovisual aids** combine sound and sight as in films and videotapes.
  E. Computer-assisted presentational aids utilize computers to generate visual and audiovisual aids.

TEACHING/LEARNING OBJECTIVES

After reading Chapter 16, your students should:

- Feel inspired and motivate to experience *ganas*.

- Aim to incorporate some persuasive appeals in their informative messages.

- Plan to incorporate as many as possible of the strategies for effective informative speaking mentioned in *Dimensions of Communication*.

- Plan to appeal to diverse learning styles in their upcoming presentation.

- Feel more confident at evaluating the numerous informative messages we are bombarded with daily.

- Feel more confident at creating and evaluating presentational aids.

- Meet the learning objectives listed on page 417 in the text.

TROUBLESHOOTING

One of the most frequent complaints instructors will hear from students is that they are having trouble selecting a topic. In fact, students often spend so much time searching for a topic that they lose valuable time that is needed for researching, organizing, and practicing. Although it requires class time, instructors and students alike may benefit in engaging in some topic brainstorming activities. Weak speech topics will ultimately undermine the student's performance and bore the instructor, who must listen to countless speeches. Another potential problem area revolves around topic duplication. Countless speeches on Olestra, the food pyramid, and the benefits of exercise will become monotonous for you and your students. It may be wise to have students sign up for topics to avoid repetition.

INSTRUCTIONAL EXERCISES

1. If time permits, show the award-winning film *Stand and Deliver*. Have students divide into their assigned small groups to discuss the main character, Jaime Escalante, in terms of his ability to inform and persuade his audience. Have each group create a list of the reasons why they believe Escalante was so successful at teaching his students.

2. Collect samples of visual aids. Break students into their assigned small groups and give each group three or four visual aids to evaluate. Using Chapter 16 as a foundation, ask students to determine the strengths and weaknesses of the aids. As a group, have students present their examples and evaluations to the class.

JOURNAL WRITING

[If you require that students videotape each of their speeches, journal entries become an excellent opportunity for self-evaluation.] Review your informative speech on your videotape. Answer the following questions regarding your presentation:

- Based on what you have learned from *Dimensions of Communication* and class lectures, what do you believe to be your strengths as a public speaker? Cite specific examples as evidence.

- Based on what you observed, what do you believe are your weaknesses? Cite specific examples as evidence.

- What do you plan to do differently in preparing for and presenting your persuasive speech?

DISCUSSION TOPICS

Lead a discussion of differences in learning styles as outlined in the chapter. Ask students to reflect on their own preferred learning style. Discuss the importance of understanding differences in learning styles in developing effective informative presentations.

Consider the numerous and varied informative messages that we receive on a daily basis. What elements seem to make these messages most effective and memorable? Compare student lists to ideas presented in Chapter 16.

Scott and Brydon discuss a variety of visual aids. Traditional types of visual aids include (a) objects, (b) models, (c) photographs, (d) diagrams and illustrations, and (e) charts, graphs, and maps. These can be constructed from a variety of materials including (a) poster board, (b) flip charts, (c) overhead transparencies, (d) slides, (e) handouts, and (f) chalkboards. In addition, Scott and Brydon introduce the idea of computer-generated presentational aids. These aids are created using computer applications and are often multimedia presentations. Discuss differences between traditional and computer-generated aids in regard to the speaker's image, credibility, and overall effectiveness.

TEST QUESTIONS

Multiple Choice

1. The most effective public speakers
   a. create a desire in their audience to put the information they present to constructive use.
   b. enable audience learning.
   c. relate the information presented to the needs and goals of the audience.
   *d. all of the above
   Page: 418

2. All of the following are learning styles EXCEPT
   a. auditory numerical.
   b. oral expressive.
   *c. cognitive-affective.
   d. individual.
   Page: 420

3. The purely mental component of learning is referred to as
   a. kinesthetic.
   b. expressive-affective.
   *c. cognition.
   d. attitudinal-affective.
   Page: 420

4. The acquisition of new information is
   a. learning.
   b. the purpose of an informative speech.
   *c. both a and b
   d. neither a nor b
   Page: 420

5. _____ is the emotional component of learning.
   a. Cognition
   *b. Affect
   c. Attitude
   d. Expressiveness
   Page: 420

6. _____ is the skill component of learning.
   a. Cognition
   *b. Behavior
   c. Affect
   d. Kinesthetics
   Page: 421

7. Which statement do some communication scholars agree with?
   a. Informative speeches also include persuasive messages.
   b. Informative speeches are and should be exclusively informative.
   *c. both a and b
   d. neither a nor b
   Page: 422

8. According to the authors of your text, the relationship between an informative and persuasive speech is
   a. a dichotomy.
   *b. a continuum.
   c. a constant source of confusion for audiences.
   d. interdependent.
   Page: 422

9. Which of the following influence(s) your opinion of an informative speech?
   a. the speaker
   b. the topic
   c. the novelty of the message
   *d. all of the above
   Page: 423

10. The audience's perception of the relevance of a speaker's message hinges on which of the following?
    a. trialability
    b. relative advantage
    *c. timeliness
    d. all of the above
    Page: 423

11. The attribute of novelty refers to information that the audience considers
    *a. new and stimulating.
    b. obscure.
    c. fashionable.
    d. all of the above
    Page: 423

12. Which message attribute concerns the appropriateness of your informative speech to audience members' attitudes, beliefs, and values?
    *a. compatibility
    b. observability
    c. trialability
    d. implementation
    Page: 424

13. Relative advantage refers to
    a. the degree to which the information can be seen by the audience.
    *b. the perception that a message is beneficial.
    c. both a and b
    d. neither a nor b
    Page: 426

14. Trialability refers to
    a. the perception that a message has some beneficial use for audience members.
    b. the opportunity to explore a message from a variety of perspectives.
    c. the process of demonstrating the benefits of constructively using the information presented in an informative speech.
    *d. the opportunity to experiment with an idea without penalty.
    Page: 427

15. Which of the following is (are) effective way(s) to inform an audience?
    a. explain
    b. describe
    c. demonstrate
    *d. all of the above
    Page: 428

16. Speeches that demonstrate differ from those that instruct in that
    *a. demonstration speeches include elements of observability and trialability.
    b. instructional speeches lack novelty.
    c. instructional speeches have greater potential for comprehensibility.
    d. all of the above
    Page: 430

17. If you plan to use a photograph in your speech, be sure to
    *a. enlarge it so that it is visible to everyone.
    b. pass it around for everyone to see.
    c. both a and b are acceptable.
    d. neither a nor b is acceptable.
    Page: 435

18. Which of the following types of visual aids would best illustrate the number of vegetable servings the average American consumes on a daily basis compared to the number of recommended servings?
    a. illustration
    b. pie chart
    c. line graph
    *d. bar chart
    Page: 437

19. Which of the following types of visual aids would best illustrate the proportion of men to women in executive positions in Fortune 500 companies?
    *a. pie chart
    b. line graph
    c. bar chart
    d. matrix
    Page: 437

20. If a speaker wants to demonstrate the steady increase in the average college freshman's SAT scores, he or she should create a
    a. pie chart.
    *b. line graph.
    c. bar chart.
    d. matrix.
    Page: 437

21. To ensure that your audience will be able to read an overhead transparency, it should be readable by the naked eye from what distance?
    a. 25 feet
    b. 15 feet
    *c. 10 feet
    d. 5 feet
    Page: 441

22. How many ideas should be included on a single visual aid?
    *a. one
    b. two
    c. no more than three
    d. as many as will fit in a legible manner
    Page: 443

23. What is the maximum number of lines that should be included on each visual aid?
    a. 2 or 3
    *b. 6 or 7
    c. 10 to 12
    d. no more than 20
    Page: 443

24. Transparencies should include information in a point size no smaller than
    a. 8.
    b. 14.
    *c. 18.
    d. 24.
    Page: 443

25. If you include videotape in your speech, a good rule of thumb is
    a. no more than 30 seconds for a 10-minute speech.
    *b. no more than 1 minute for a 10-minute speech.
    c. no more than 1 minute for a 5-minute speech.
    d. none of the above
    Page: 445

True/False

26. *Ganas* refers to someone's ability to creatively produce visual aids. (False, p. 417)

27. Cognition refers to the purely mental component of learning. (True, p. 420)

28. In essence, a good lecture is an effective informative speech. (True, p. 421)

29. The perception of novelty heightens selective exposure. (True, p. 423)

30. Relative advantage refers to the likelihood that a speaker will be effective at informing or persuading his or her audience. (False, p. 425)

Short Answer/Essay

31. Explain the concept of *ganas*. (p. 417)

32. Explain why audience learning styles are important to a public speaker. List some strategies for effectively appealing to these different styles. (p. 418)

33. When does an informative speech become a persuasive one? (p. 421)

34. Explain the idea of the informative-persuasive continuum. (p. 421)

35. List and explain the six attributes a message should possess in order to increase the likelihood of being perceived as relevant by the audience. (p. 423)

CHAPTER 17
PERSUASIVE SPEAKING

INTRODUCTION AND OUTLINE

Chapter 17 provides students with a basic theoretical understanding of the persuasion process and practical suggestions for creating and delivering an effective persuasive speech. Specifically, the chapter discusses:

I. Sarah Brady's story illustrates the process of preparing and delivering an effective persuasive speech.

II. Persuading your audience

    A. Audience-focused persuasive speaking requires a clear understanding of your goals as a speaker, knowledge about your audience, and an assessment of the constraints facing you, including the ethical boundaries you must stay within.

    B. The four common goals of persuasive speaking include

        1. to reinforce the attitudes, beliefs, and values an audience already holds;

        2. to inoculate an audience against counterpersuasion;

        3. to change attitudes; and

        4. to prompt action.

            a. This is the most difficult goal to achieve.

            b. A foundation must first be laid that will make the audience likely to act.

    C. The realization of any of these goals depends upon how well the speaker has analyzed the audience.

        1. Audience analysis starts with an assessment of the relationship between the audience and the speaker's goals. Not all audiences are capable of acting to help speakers achieve their goals, even if they desire to do so.

        2. Adequate audience analysis also requires the speaker to consider the three levels of diversity discussed in Chapter 7: cultural, group, and individual.

    D. Ethical constraints suggest that the realization of your persuasive goal should not come at the expense of your audience. The end you hope to achieve must reflect not only your interests, but also those of your audience.

III. Roots of persuasive speaking

    A. Most contemporary theory and research about persuasive speaking grows out of the observations of the philosopher Aristotle.

    B. Aristotle identified three means of persuasion: ethos, logos, and pathos. These three correspond to the three basic elements of any persuasive speech situation: speaker, message, and audience.

        1. **Ethos** refers to the credibility of a speaker.

            a. Aristotle described ethos as a combination of competence and character which is essential to a speaker's chance of persuading an audience.

            b. Today's scholars use the term **source credibility**, which is the audience's perception of the speaker's believability.

        2. **Logos** is the proof a speaker offers to an audience through the words of his or her message.

            a. Logos is the Greek word for "word."

        b. Aristotle believed speakers should use logical proof including the syllogism and enthymeme.

    3. **Pathos** refers to the emotional states that a speaker can arouse in an audience and use to achieve persuasive goals.

        a. These methods are not inherently unethical, but they can be abused by unscrupulous persuaders.

        b. Specific emotions Aristotle mentioned in his writings include anger, fear, kindness, shame, pity, and envy.

IV. The speaker: Persuasion through ethos

    A. Contemporary communication research shows that the perception of credibility is composed of two parts: competence and character.

    B. Credibility is dynamic and changing. Thus, one of your goals is to build and maintain your credibility as you speak.

        1. Credibility before you speak

            a. Often, speakers' reputations precede their appearance before an audience.

            b. One way to build credibility before you speak is to have someone introduce you. If you do not have an introduction, you will have to establish your credibility by what you say and how you say it.

        2. Credibility during the speech

            a. Whatever credibility a speaker has before a speech may be negated by the speaker's appearance, message, and/or delivery.

            b. Speakers with little initial credibility can build ethos through (1) their appearance; (2) the care with which they've prepared their message; (3) their delivery; (4) citing their credentials or expertise; and (5) citing evidence.

        3. Credibility after the speech

            a. Once gained, credibility needs nourishment.

            b. Tips for maintaining credibility, on page 459, include:

        1. Ask yourself about the degree to which your audience already perceives you as credible and if you have provided them with any reason to change their opinion.

        2. Dress appropriately.

        3. Incorporate any expertise or experience you have.

        4. Use evidence to support the claims you make.

        5. Engage your audience nonverbally.

        6. Use inclusive language.

    C. Using similarity and dissimilarity

        1. People tend to be suspicious of people they perceive to be dissimilar and initially trusting of people they perceive as similar.

        2. Similarity is a perception composed chiefly of appearance, background, and belief system.

        3. Similarity and dissimilarity can both work to your advantage and disadvantage.

        4. You can use similarity and dissimilarity to increase the audience's perceptions of your credibility.

V. The message: Persuasion through logos

    A. What you put into your persuasive message and how you structure it are crucial to the success of meeting your persuasive goal.

B. To build a successful persuasive message, you need (1) a model of argument you can use as a template for your message; (2) understanding of how to use this model with evidence and reasoning; and (3) understanding of the extent to which you should include both sides of a controversial issue in your message.

1. The Toulmin model, introduced first in Chapter 6 and explained in further detail in Chapter 17, provides students with a model to (1) critically assess the persuasive messages of others and (2) follow to develop their own persuasive speeches.

    a. Key parts of this model, explained on pages 464–466, include the claim, grounds, warrant, backing, rebuttal qualifier, first-order data, second-order data, and third-order data.

    b. A list of the kinds of questions the model encourages is found on page 467 and includes:

       (1) What is the nature of the claims I am making?

       (2) What kind of evidence do I need to offer in support of my claim? First-, second-, or third-order data? All three? How will the evidence I offer influence perceptions of my credibility?

       (3) What can I do to make certain that my audience will make the connection between the claim I make and the evidence I offer as grounds in support of it? Is the warrant really so obvious that I don't need to make it explicitly for my audience?

       (4) Will the warrant need additional support in the form of backing to be acceptable to my audience?

C. The importance of two-sided messages

1. A two-sided message is more effective than a one-sided one.

    a. A one-sided persuasive message offers only evidence in support of a claim.

    b. A two-sided message makes use of what Toulmin called the qualifier and the rebuttal.

2. Acknowledging opposing arguments does not mean you are abandoning your claim.

    a. Your task is to point out weaknesses in the rebuttal or the reason why the rebuttal is not sufficient to set aside your overall claim.

    b. The rebuttal represents the second side of the message.

3. In addition to being more persuasive, the two-sided message offers at least two other benefits.

    a. It enhances the speaker's credibility.

    b. It makes the audience members more resistant to counterpersuasion.

VI. The audience: Persuasion through pathos

A. Whereas logical proofs are designed to induce elaborate thinking on the part of the audience, the emotional appeals are designed to provoke audience members to respond without the benefit of such elaborated thought.

B. These appeals are linked to emotions such as anger, fear, kindness, calmness, confidence, unkindness, friendship, shame, pity, enmity, shamelessness, and envy.

C. Appealing to emotions: Motivating through fear

1. Research indicates that moderate fear is an effective motivator especially when the speaker gives audience members a set of clear-cut steps they can take to reduce fear.

2. Too much fear can diminish persuasive effects because it tends to elicit denial from the audience.
   D. Appealing to primitive beliefs, or beliefs instilled since childhood
      1. Reciprocity: When people receive a promise or are asked to return something received, the conditioned response is to reciprocate in kind.
      2. Liking: The assumption is that people can influence and persuade the people who like them.
      3. Authority: Research indicates that some people are predisposed to comply with the requests from individuals and institutions they perceive as authoritative.
      4. Social support: There is a tendency among some to believe that if enough people say it is so, it must be so.
      5. Scarcity: People are conditioned to believe that something that is scarce is valuable enough to merit their attention.
      6. Commitment: This principle tells us that we all feel pressure to keep our attitudes, beliefs, and values consistent with our commitments.

VII. Persuasive speaking in practice
   A. Adapting your goals to your audience
      1. Speeches to reinforce or inoculate presume that members are supportive of or uninformed about the topic. They are considered friendly or neutral.
      2. A speech to change attitudes, by definition, means your audience disagrees with you. This is termed a hostile audience.
      3. Speeches that prompt people to act presume either that (1) the audience has been prepared by prior messages to take action or (2) the topic is not inherently controversial.
   B. Organizing your persuasive speech
      1. Two organizational patterns, first introduced in Chapter 14, are particularly suited for persuasive efforts.
      2. The problem-solution analyzes a problem in terms of harm, significance, and cause, and then proposes a solution which is described, feasible, and advantageous.
      3. Monroe's motivated sequence organizes material in five steps which include (1) attention, (2) need, (3) satisfaction, (4) visualization, and (5) action.
      4. Regardless of the plan you choose, follow these two principles:
         a. Put your best arguments and support at the beginning or end; don't hide them in the middle.
         b. With hostile or indifferent audiences, it is particularly important to have some of your best material early in the speech.
   C. Balancing the means of persuasion
      1. Ethos, pathos, and logos are not separate, but work together as means of persuasion.
      2. A good persuasive speech relies on the speaker, message, and audience for its success.
   D. Answering good questions
      1. Frequently after delivering a persuasive speech, you will be expected to answer questions.
      2. Some basic guidelines for handling a question-and-answer period follow.
         a. Announce at the outset that you will take questions at the end of your speech.

b. Overprepare for your speech.

c. Restate questions if they can't be heard by all.

d. Answer questions directly with facts to back up your answers.

e. Take questions from different audience members.

f. Be brief.

g. Announce when you are near the end of the Q&A.

h. At the end of the Q&A, be sure to restate the focus of your speech and summarize its essential points.

TEACHING/LEARNING OBJECTIVES

After reading Chapter 17, students should:

- Recognize that persuasion is all around us and as a result we need to be critical thinkers.

- Recognize the differences between practicing ethical and unethical persuasion.

- Commit to considering the needs of their audience when creating persuasive messages, both in and out of the classroom.

- Plan to incorporate the strategies for effective persuasive speaking mentioned in *Dimensions of Communication* in their upcoming assignment.

- Meet the learning objectives listed on page 451 in the text.

TROUBLESHOOTING

Inevitably, some students will create and deliver a speech that sounds more informative than persuasive. Or at the other extreme, some students will aim to change audiences' fundamental values in a single eight-minute-or-so speech. Then, there are those students who insist on beating a dead horse topic one more time just in case the audience hasn't heard it all before. To avoid all of these scenarios, spend time discussing appropriate persuasive topics. Use the topic selection criteria presented in Chapter 14, on page 354, as a starting point for discussion. Perhaps engage the class in a brainstorming activity which creates *class* criteria for topics and/or a list of topics not allowed. Using this method, instructors can ensure that just because they have heard a recycling speech a thousand times, they don't prohibit speech topics that students would find worthwhile.

INSTRUCTIONAL EXERCISES

1. Two-sided messages require that students create a rebuttal, which is an exception to or a refutation of the argument. In essence, a rebuttal statement is the "But, what about ---?" statement. Break students into groups of three. Provide each student with a controversial topic which they are to create a claim and grounds for. Give students about five minutes to complete this task. Students should then take turns announcing their claim or position and the reasons or evidence. Other group members are to ask, "But what about ---?" to show the speaker areas that would need to be developed to effectively create a persuasive two-sided message.

2. Break students into small groups of three or four or their assigned small groups. Ask students to come up with a 2–3-minute "sales pitch" speech. Students must use at least one of the primitive appeals and include a two-sided message. The group is to select a "salesperson" who will present the speech to the class.

3. Have students bring an advertisement to class that incorporates any of the persuasive appeals discussed in Chapter 17. In small groups, have students share and discuss their advertisements and collectively decide which example best exemplifies persuasion in practice. The owner of the selected advertisement can either choose to explain to the audience the persuasion process (for participation points) or choose another groupmate to present in his or her place (for participation points).

JOURNAL WRITING

Like communication competence, effective persuasion is dependent upon truly understanding your audience. Consider past experiences in which you tried to persuade someone unsuccessfully to your point of view, to act on your behalf, or to act in a way that benefits you. Recount this experience from your point of view. What was your goal? What strategies did you employ? What did you appeal to? Now recount this same experience from the other person's point of view. In your attempt to persuade, what did you overlook or fail to consider?

DISCUSSION TOPICS

History is rich with examples of people who were effective at using persuasion to reach unethical, and often inhumane, ends. Ask students to come up with a few such cases. Next, ask students to think of those who have used effective persuasion to benefit society. Engage the class in a discussion regarding whether or not they believe anyone has the right, or is acting ethically, when they attempt to prompt action or impose their views on another. Under what circumstances, if any, is such behavior warranted? Who decides what is ethical and what is unethical?

As a class, brainstorm everyday instances in which someone is trying to persuade us. Keep a list on the board. Use this list to discuss (1) how persuasion is all around us; (2) the informative-persuasive continuum of messages; and (3) the variety of appeals that would-be persuaders use.

Discuss the applicability of Aristotle's ethos-pathos-logos model to contemporary persuasion. Using examples of televised advertising by celebrities, ask students to discuss how ethos is currently used in selling products. Using anti–drug abuse ads, AIDS awareness, and the like, discuss the use of emotions such as fear and hope to persuade. Finally, discuss how logical arguments and the words of ads are used to persuade. By the end of the discussion, students should be able to see examples of all three elements of the Aristotelian model in contemporary persuasion.

TEST QUESTIONS

Multiple Choice

1. Persuasive speaking requires
    a. a clear understanding of your goals as a speaker.
    b. an assessment of the constraints facing you.
    c. an understanding of your ethical boundaries.
    *d. all of the above
    Page: 452

2. Which of the following are goals of persuasive speaking?
    a. to reinforce existing attitudes, beliefs, and values
    b. to inoculate an audience
    c. to change attitudes and/or behavior
    *d. all of the above
    Pages: 452–453

3. The most difficult persuasive goal to achieve is
    a. changing attitudes.
    *b. prompting behavior.
    c. demonstrating the benefits of accepting your position.
    d. All of the above are equally challenging.
    Page: 454

4. When people seem to be responding to a single persuasive speech, it is likely that
    a. they were predisposed to act.
    b. they are probably listening to a message that is part of a long history of messages.
    *c. both a and b
    d. neither a nor b
    Page: 454

5. When you inoculate an audience, you
    a. hope to reinforce strong commitments to a position or behavior.
    *b. hope to reinforce existing attitudes, beliefs, values, and behaviors to avoid counterpersuasion.
    c. repeat a similar message in many forms and styles in an effort to change basic values over a period of time.
    d. none of the above
    Page: 454

6. If an audience is similar to the speaker,
    a. a speech of inoculation is called for.
    b. an informative speech, not a persuasive speech, is called for.
    c. a speech which promotes action is required.
    *d. none of the above
    Page: 454

7. When analyzing an audience, speakers need to consider all of the following EXCEPT
   a. the three levels of audience diversity.
   b. the fact that not all audiences will be capable of helping a speaker meet his or her goals.
   *c. the fact that most audiences are not receptive to the idea that someone is trying to persuade them.
   d. how audience diversity might affect the construction and delivery of a speech.
   Page: 454

8. According to the authors of your text, the idea that speakers have ethical constraints is best captured in which of the following statements?
   a. The ends justify the means.
   b. Noble ends justify ignoble means.
   c. Strive for the greatest good for the greatest number.
   *d. none of the above
   Page: 455

9. Sarah Brady's persuasive speeches had what goal or goals?
   a. a change in behavior on the part of existing gun owners
   *b. legislative action
   c. reinforcing the attitudes of those who disagreed with handgun control
   d. all of the above
   Page: 456

10. Most contemporary theory and research about persuasive speaking can be traced to
    a. Socrates.
    b. Quintilion.
    c. Plato.
    *d. Aristotle.
    Page: 456

11. The three means of persuasion are
    a. the speaker, message, and audience.
    *b. ethos, pathos, and logos.
    c. beliefs, attitudes, and values.
    d. individual, group, and cultural.
    Page: 457

12. Ethos refers to
    a. the delivery style of the speaker.
    *b. the speaker's credibility.
    c. the proof that a speaker offers to his or her audience.
    d. the likely reaction of the audience.
    Page: 457

13. The combination of competence and character refers to
    a. the speaker's believability.
    b. source credibility.
    c. ethos.
    *d. all of the above
    Page: 457

14. Source credibility refers to
    *a. the audience's perception of the speaker's believability.
    b. the physical evidence that a speaker provides to support a claim.
    c. both a and b
    d. neither a nor b
    Page: 457

15. In an attempt to maintain credibility, the authors of your text suggest all of the following EXCEPT
    a. dressing appropriately for the occasion.
    b. using evidence to support your claims.
    *c. relying on your reputation.
    d. sharing special expertise or credentials.
    Page: 458

16. Which of the following parts of the Toulmin model represents evidence on which an arguer bases a claim?
    *a. grounds
    b. warrant
    c. backing
    d. qualifier
    Page: 464

17. Creating a two-sided message requires the speaker to incorporate which part of the Toulmin model?
    a. backing
    *b. rebuttal
    c. warrant
    d. first-order data
    Page: 466

18. _____ refers to the emotional state that a speaker can arouse in an audience and use to achieve persuasive goals.
    a. Ethos
    *b. Pathos
    c. Logos
    d. Empathy
    Page: 468

19. Which of the following is NOT a primitive belief?
    *a. fear
    b. liking
    c. authority
    d. commitment
    Pages: 470–472

20. Advertisers who use celebrity spokespersons attempt to appeal to
    a. authority.
    *b. liking.
    c. social support.
    d. commitment.
    Page: 470

21. An appeal based on the laws of supply and demand is
    a. reciprocity.
    b. fear.
    *c. scarcity.
    d. social support.
    Page: 472

22. According to the authors of your text, which of the following is the strongest appeal?
    a. scarcity
    b. liking
    c. authority
    *d. commitment
    Page: 472

23. Speeches to inoculate presume that
    a. audience members are already supportive.
    b. audience members are uninformed on a topic.
    *c. both a and b
    d. neither a nor b
    Page: 473

True/False

24. The realization of any persuasive goals depends largely on how well the speaker has analyzed the audience. (True, p. 454)

25. Credibility is permanent and stable. (False, p. 457)

26. Credibility can be established by way of reputation. (True, p. 458)

27. For a person to be successful at persuasion, his or her credibility must be established prior to speaking. (False, p. 459)

28. In a public speaking situation where there is little initial speaker credibility, a speaker should focus on pathos in order to be perceived as credible. (False, p. 459)

Short Answer/Essay

29. Explain the differences, and potential similarities, between ethical and unethical persuasion. (pp. 455–456)

30. Diagram and explain the Toulmin model. (pp. 464–467)

31. According to the authors or your text, the two-sided message helps to make audience members more resistant to counterpersuasion. Explain the notion of a two-sided message and why the authors believe it provides speakers with this benefit. (pp. 467–468)

32. What are primitive beliefs and how are they important to the process of persuasion? List and explain each belief. (pp. 470–472)

33. In many instances, speakers will have an opportunity to answer questions from the audience regarding their speech. What basic guidelines do the authors of your text provide for handling the Q&A? (pp. 476–477)

CHAPTER 18
MASS COMMUNICATION

INTRODUCTION AND OUTLINE

Chapter 18 provides a thorough overview of the historical development of mass media and the competing theories which explore its influence. Specifically, the chapter discusses:

I. The nature of mass communication
   A. Mass communication (1) involves one source transmitting a message to an audience and (2) uses devices to facilitate communication between sources and audience members that are physically separated.
   B. Mass communication differs from face-to-face communication in terms of its audience, its response to feedback, and the degree to which mass communication is subject to regulation.
   C. The audience
      1. Mediated systems of communication, like chat rooms on the Internet, enable senders to pinpoint their desired audience.
      2. Traditional mass communication systems, such as network television, target the largest possible audience.
         a. Because broadcasters cannot respond immediately to the feedback from the audience, they cannot adapt their messages for some time.
         b. The goal of the producers of mass communication content is to appeal to as many people as possible.
   D. Feedback
      1. Feedback in mediated communication, regardless of whether it is instant or delayed, is one-on-one. The sender of the message knows who is providing the feedback.
         a. Mediated systems like telephones and Internet chat rooms provide instantaneous feedback.
         b. E-mail feedback is mediated but requires delayed feedback.
      2. In mass communication, feedback is almost always delayed.
         a. Feedback, like ratings and box-office sales, is not identifiable on an individual basis.
         b. Some feedback might be individual, such as calls to a station or letters to the editor, but this feedback may not be representative of the entire audience.
   E. Regulation
      1. The content of communication over mediated systems is largely unregulated. However, there are a few restrictions on material transmitted to children over the Internet.
      2. In the United States, electronic media is highly regulated by the Federal Communications Commission.

a. Although protected by the First Amendment, print media can be subject to regulation of obscenity and pornography.

b. Libel laws allow individuals to sue those who publish or broadcast defamatory stories.

II. History of mass communication (refer to Figure 18-1, on pages 486–487, for greater detail)

A. The evolution of print media

1. Writing was invented between 5000 and 4000 B.C.

2. The Egyptians developed paper from papyrus around 3000 B.C.

3. By the second century A.D., paper as we know it was developed in China.

4. In Europe, paper became the medium of choice for early books, which were copied by hand.

5. Gutenberg invented movable type in 1455, which led to the forms of print media we currently enjoy.

6. Newspapers reached their high in 1910; readership has declined since.

7. Electronic media and magazine publishing continue to grow.

B. The evolution of electronic media

1. The movies

a. The first electronic mass medium of communication was the motion picture.

b. The motion picture was made possible by George Eastman, who developed the film that creates the illusion of movement.

c. The first movie theaters were called nickelodeons, and they showed silent movies.

d. The 1930s and 1940s were the golden age of movies.

e. Television was invented and movie attendance dropped.

f. To meet the challenges of TV, movies began to have more relaxed codes about what could be shown.

2. Radio

a. In 1844 Samuel Morse successfully transmitted the first telegraph message.

b. By 1895 messages were sent by wireless telegraph, the radio.

c. In 1906 the first human voice was sent wireless.

d In 1920 the first amateur broadcast began.

e. Congress passed the Radio Act of 1927 and the Federal Communications Act of 1934.

3. Television

a. After World War II, television began to preempt radio as the nation's favorite medium.

b. The first experimental broadcast of television occurred in the 1920s.

c. By 1936 there were test broadcasts, but they were interrupted by WWII.

d. After the war, sets were manufactured and sold to the wealthy.

e. When television licenses were unfrozen in 1952, the boom in TV began.

III. Functions and effects of mass communication

A. There are a number of competing ideas and theories about the effects of mass communication.

1. Direct effects
   a. Many believe that the mass media powerfully and directly affect the behavior of the people in their audience (Figure 18-3). Yet, the magic bullet theory does not stand up to scientific scrutiny.
   b. The **two-step flow** (Figure 18-4) of media influence suggests ideas flow from media to opinion leaders and from them to the general population. In short, it suggest the media has, at most, minimal effects.
2. **Uses and gratifications**
   a. This theory suggests that the audience members' reasons for consuming media messages and the gratifications they seek affect how they process the messages. Thus, communication represents a transaction between the source who provides a message and the audience member who uses it.
   b. Unlike earlier, direct-effect models, which cast audience members in a passive role, the uses and gratifications model assumes audience members are active and making conscious choices about the media they consume.
3. Agenda setting
   a. The basic premise of the **agenda-setting** hypothesis is that although the media might not tell the audience what to think, they could have a significant impact on what audience members think about.
   b. Research indicates that the media is more powerful with some issues than with others.
      (1) Unobtrusive issues that the average person has little familiarity with have the greatest agenda-setting effects, and vice versa.
      (2) Furthermore, the greater uncertainty audiences have about an issue or a situation, the more they will seek out information about it from the media.
4. Theories about mass communication and culture
   a. The **social construction of reality theory** suggests that people create a symbolic reality that is as influential as physical reality.
      (1) This socially constructed reality is a result of mass and interpersonal communication.
      (2) This idea is similar to agenda setting with the difference that rather than simply determining how a list of issues is prioritized, media are seen as actually affecting public attitudes and behaviors through their portrayals of the reality in which we live.
   b. **Cultivation analysis** is a theory that suggests that the world view of heavy consumers of mass media is influenced by the predominant perspectives and themes of media programming.
   c. **Critical perspectives** are various perspectives that deal with the fundamental issue of power and its relationship to communication.
      (1) **Critical theory** is a critical perspective based on the theories of Karl Marx and Sigmund Freud, which hold that the elites use mass media to sustain their privileged positions in society.
      (2) The **cultural studies approach** is a perspective that argues that mass media are used so that the ruling class can impose its thinking on the working class.

IV. You and mass media
   A. Become a critical consumer of mass communication.
      1. Ask yourself what messages are being presented and what vision of reality is implied by the media.
      2. Apply the same tests of critical thinking that you apply to interpersonal and public speaking to the mass media.
      3. Become a conscious consumer of the media.
   B. Know the issues of concern.
      1. Media bias: Is there a liberal or conservative bias in the media?
      2. Violence and the media: Do the media actually incite the violence they portray?
      3. Freedom of speech: What limits are appropriate?

TEACHING/LEARNING OBJECTIVES

After reading Chapter 18, students should:

- Appreciate the inventions and technological advancements that led us to the mass media we enjoy and study today.

- Understand the competing theories that suggest the degree of influence mass communication wields.

- Reflect on their use of mass communication and the degree to which they believe it influences their lives.

- Recognize individual instances where mass communication has influenced their thinking, opinion, or decision.

- Recognize the importance of becoming a critical and conscious consumer of the media.

- Understand the issues and debates that revolve around mass communication.

- Meet the learning objectives listed on page 481 in the text.

TROUBLESHOOTING

Chapter 18, as the final chapter of the text, must be digested by students in a relatively short period of time, regardless of whether you operate on the semester or quarter system. Scott and Brydon present the material in an unambiguous and organized fashion, but a thorough review of mass communication is complex and time-consuming. The fact that this chapter's material is likely to be introduced at the end of the term, when students and instructors alike are preparing for exams, can be a problem. But, then again, shortness of time and energy poses a potential problem regardless of what subject area you discuss last. An instructor's challenge is to make Chapter 18 as exciting and fresh as Chapter 1.

INSTRUCTIONAL EXERCISES

1. Print, radio, television, and the Internet can all potentially provide students with valuable information on the day's events. Ask students to choose a topic that is currently being discussed in the media that is of particular interest to them, but one

about which they know little. Ask students to search, over a period of a couple of days, each of the above media for their topic and determine if they receive the same "picture" of the event from all. Ask students to prepare a 3–4-minute speech to report their findings. This speech should follow all of the guidelines for creating and delivering an effective speech that have been discussed during the term.

2. There is an ongoing debate over whether or not the media is biased despite journalists' goal of remaining objective. The debate also revolves around whether there is a liberal or conservative bias. Have students bring in samples of media coverage that claim objectivity (e.g., newspapers or newsweekly magazines) but clearly include bias.

JOURNAL WRITING

Most of us have a favorite show that we always try to make time to watch. Consider "your" show and why you think that it is your favorite. Specifically consider (1) why you watch it; (2) what you learn from it, if anything; and (3) in what ways it influences your behavior or view of the world.

DISCUSSION TOPICS

E-mail has replaced the telephone and traditional penned letter for many people. Discuss the advantages and disadvantages of this new method of communication.

Chapter 18 discusses the debate over the degree of influence the media has on its audience. Consider your own experiences with the media and how it has influenced you. Be specific. For example, is your hairstyle or clothing style influenced by images seen on television? Did you change your decision on who you will vote for in the next election based on something you saw or heard? Write down at least three areas of your life that have been influenced by the media, no matter how insignificant or meaningless they might seem. Have students share their lists and discuss the pervasiveness of the media's influence, the vast areas of our lives that the media touches, and the individual varying levels of influence that the media seems to have.

The First Amendment guarantees freedom of speech. Yet, there are laws in place which sometimes regulate what can and cannot be said or shown. Engage the class in a discussion regarding whether or not they believe there should be limits on freedom of speech.

TEST QUESTIONS

Multiple Choice

1. Mass communication differs from face-to-face communication in that
   *a. feedback on mass communication is less immediate.
   b. mass communication requires there to be a large audience.
   c. mass communication is largely unregulated.
   d. none of the above
   Page: 482

2. Traditional mass communication systems are characterized by all of the following EXCEPT that
    a. sources and audiences are physically separated.
    b. a device or medium is required to facilitate communication.
    *c. mass communication focuses on pinpointing an audience with very specific, predetermined characteristics.
    d. none of the above
    Page: 482

3. Feedback in mediated systems differs from feedback in mass communication systems in that
    a. feedback in mediated systems is always instant.
    *b. feedback in mass communication systems is not typically identifiable.
    c. feedback in mass communication systems is always delayed.
    d. all of the above
    Page: 484

4. Ticket sales and ratings
    a. are methods used to determine advertising dollars.
    b. are instant methods of audience feedback.
    *c. both a and b
    d. neither a nor b
    Page: 485

5. Paper, as we know it, was developed by
    a. the Egyptians.
    *b. the Chinese.
    c. the Greeks.
    d. the Romans.
    Page: 485

6. Movable type was invented around
    a. 1100 A.D.
    *b. 1400 A.D.
    c. 1600 A.D.
    d. 1800 A.D.
    Page: 485

7. Movable type was invented by
    a. Aristotle.
    *b. Gutenberg.
    c. Morse.
    d. McLuhan.
    Page: 485

8. Freedom of the press is protected under
    a. the Fifth Amendment.
    *b. the First Amendment.
    c. the Federal Communications Act.
    d. the preamble to the U.S. Constitution.
    Page: 485

9. The first electronic medium of communication was
   a. the telephone.
   *b. motion picture film.
   c. radio.
   d. wireless radio.
   Page: 489

10. The first movie theaters were
    a. designed for the upper and middle classes.
    *b. called nickelodeons.
    c. unsuccessful.
    d. none of the above
    Page: 489

11. In 1844 which significant event took place that influenced the development of mass communication?
    a. movable type was invented.
    *b. Samuel Morse successfully transmitted the first telegraph message.
    c. The Constitution was amended to include the right to freedom of speech.
    d. George Eastman invented film that created the illusion of motion.
    Page: 489

12. People who serve as conduits for media influence, directly influencing those less concerned about political issues, are known as
    a. gatekeepers.
    b. spokespeople.
    *c. opinion leaders.
    d. social constructionists.
    Page: 494

13. The theory which assumes an audience is active and consciously choosing which media to consume is
    a. social construction of reality.
    *b. uses and gratifications.
    c. agenda setting.
    d. cultivation analysis.
    Page: 496

14. The media's ability to determine the issues of public debate by choosing which events to report and which to ignore is best known as
    a. the social construction of reality.
    *b. agenda setting.
    c. the societal studies approach.
    d. the two-step flow approach.
    Page: 497

15. Critical perspectives typically deal with
    a. demonstrating to media consumers the benefits of critical thinking when receiving media messages.
    *b. fundamental issues of power and its relationship to communication.
    c. comparing and contrasting competing theories regarding the influence of mass media on audiences.
    d. none of the above
    Page: 502

True/False

16. Mediated communication systems, like mass communication systems, typically experience delayed audience feedback. (False, p. 484)

17. George Eastman invented photography. (False, p. 489)

18. Opinion leaders are defined as those most likely to set the media's agenda. (False, p. 494)

19. Research indicates that people who watch a great deal of TV have exaggerated perceptions of crime rates. (True, p. 501)

20. Surveys of "elite" reporters, from papers such as the *New York Times* and *Washington Post*, found them to be more conservative and likely to vote for a conservative candidate. (False, p. 506)

Short Answer/Essay

21. Mediated communication varies from mass communication in a number of ways. List and explain at least three major differences. (p. 482)

22. Pick one area of mass communication, print, radio, or television, and list the major events of its evolution. (pp. 485–482)

23. The authors of your text explain a number of communication theories that help us to understand the media's influence or lack thereof. Pick one theory and explain it thoroughly. Next, state whether you agree with the assumptions of this theory and the findings it suggests. (pp. 498–504)

24. The authors of your text suggest that consumers of mass media be aware of the issues of concern among communication scholars. What are the three issues that the authors specifically suggest students be aware of? (p. 510)

25. In your opinion, do the media incite the violence they portray? Provide specific examples to support your position. (pp. 500–502)